Make Music With

Radiohead

Complete Lyrics / Guitar Chord Boxes & Symbols / Guide To Guitar Tablature
Fifteen classic songs with a foreword by Stevie Chick

D1127336

Published 2003

© International Music Publications Ltd
Griffin House 161 Hammersmith Road London W6 8BS England

Editor: Chris Harvey
Foreword: Stevie Chick
Design: Dominic Brookman
Music arranged and engraved by: Artemis Music Ltd
Cover Photograph: Dan Holdsworth with kind permission of Courtyard Music
All other photography: John Super, Ebet Roberts, Patrick Ford, Michael Linssen, Mick Hutson: Redferns Music Pucture Library / mirrorpix.com

Foreword

Rock'n'roll* has always been the preserve of the misfits and the oddballs.

*[and whatever crazed, beautiful shapes Radiohead have pulled electric noise into throughout their epochal career, we'll call it rock'n'roll, because Radiohead defy such broad definition]

Sometimes those misfits and oddballs translate their sense of displacement into a rock'n'roll that denies their disenfranchisement. In the arena of rock'n'roll, they drown whatever caused the mainstream to spurn them in the first place, a cranked amp and a surge of guitar transforming them into figureheads for worship by the very people that, in everyday life, rejected them. Still displaced, then, but through rock'n'roll, and the cult of personality that attends the culture, they ascend to the head of some republican monarchy; rock'n'roll the pole-vault that launches them into this rarefied space.

Other times, however, those oddballs and misfits enrobe their singularity with jagged noise, scarringly personal inflection, and an intolerance of the way things are. Some try to change the world about them until it fits them better, others lead by example and spin their oddity off into ever deeper and more remarkable flights of artistic fancy that charm others to follow them. They pull the mainstream in their direction, displace the displacers, find salvation and society in whatever made them 'special'.

Radiohead, defiantly, belong in that second group. They've never conformed. They've never been satisfied with music 'as is', always pushing the boundaries, tugging at rock's limitations until it fits *them*, and not the other way around. Same with a music industry seemingly designed to confound free, creative spirits like themselves. Radiohead never played ball, and stuck to their guns safe in the knowledge that the sheer quality of the music they were carving - visionary, emotionally-charged, (whisper it) progressive - would draw an audience even though it couldn't easily be sublimated into a popular culture busy squandering its attention span on trivia and nonsense.

Radiohead's refusal to compromise their vision is the key, in many ways, to their success. Their's is a singular brand of musical exploration, not without its influences - though these are intelligently filtered and creatively worked upon - and not without its followers (though many of these choose just a single facet of Radiohead's polyphonic spree to explore, remaining single-dimensional siphons at the font of Radiohead's example for their entire careers).

Their purposeful ignorance of the facile trends and momentary foibles of the music industry and its narrow-minded view of 'what people want' means that their sonic experiments and emotive flailings have scooped up whole portions of the music audience left cold by the mainstream. Their melding of unfamiliar and unfashionable slivers of musics past, present and future has resulted in an amalgam of aural possibilities and imaginations that sounds, simultaneously, completely new and utterly right.

They almost single-handedly took prog-rock from the critic's bad-books and restored the genre's lost pride, concentrating on its very progressiveness - the sense of musical ambition and creativity that was roundly gobbed-upon after punk-rock's savage year-zero politiks tossed out the baby of prog-rock's hunger and ribald aestheticism along with the bathwater that was the genre's penchant for noodly muso-ism and tiresome Tolkeinesque lyrical concerns - and placing that sensibility within a totally modern musical setting.

And it is Radiohead's progressive musical sensibility that is screamingly apparent throughout each and every one of their releases. Their creative arc is as impressive as it is easily traceable - each album is a coherent, apparent step forward from its predecessor; the electroid twitches and post-production swirls of **Kid A** and **Amnesiac** must've seemed unimaginable to the fans piqued by the searing emo-rock of **Pablo Honey**, but those who followed the journey step by step, and weren't lost by Radiohead's refusal to stand in the same spot for longer than was absolutely necessary, would've found their way to these pinnacles of triumphant creativity with ease, not a foot misplaced.

Anyone Can Play Guitar was the snotty declaration Radiohead spat forth on their indignant debut album, and it seems to sum up the band's ethos utterly. Yeah, anyone *can* play guitar, and a cursory glance round at their contemporaries must've confirmed for Radiohead that, just as it was all too easy to strap on a six-stringer and lay forth some notes that fumbled at an approximation of your soul, it was all too easy to be a rock-star. Plenty of unworthy do-nothings posing at being musicians without testing the limits of their selves, their roles, their abilities as artists.

That wouldn't be Radiohead's path. Theirs has been a career of artful contrariness, testing and then demolishing boundaries, pushing the envelope sonically, lyrically and conventionally. And, in the wake of their beautiful noise, their carefully-crafted screeds, would follow a dedicated cadre of fans, whose passion for Radiohead's twisting route would - at the height of the hysteria surrounding their **Kid A** album especially - make a mockery of the music industry's claims that the heartlands of rock fandom were possessed of an appetite unable to digest such weighty, varied and potent fare.

Quiet revolutionaries, then. In that their assault on conventions of taste and received wisdom in the music world has never been for its own sake, only through their own artistic desires, and following their creative impulses to their illogical conclusions, not a word wasted and not a note squandered. A career garlanded with deserved superlatives, changing and touching all those it encounters. And this could feasibly be just the beginning.

But for the *actual* beginning of Radiohead's story, we have to repair to the boys' hometown of Oxford. It was here they met, as students of Abingdon School. It was here that the band-members met, a strange scattered few who nevertheless connected on a most profound, productive level.

There was, of course, Thom Yorke. The future-guitarist/vocalist and troubled pin-up for a similarly troubled generation, Thom was born with a paralysed eye. A sequence of operations over the first six years of his life restored his eyesight, but he retained a squint and a lazy eye as a result, though the typically reticent Yorke would never suggest that this malady made him any kind of an outcast at school. He would, however, later admit that his over-riding ambition as a child was to be a popstar. With a wry cynicism, he explained that his affinity for pop music derived from the fact that it was "one of the few artforms that can actually pay well. And I love it more than anything," he belatedly added. Thom's love of music was compounded by the gift of a Spanish guitar from his parents, when he was 8 years old, shortly after the family moved to the Thames Valley.

At school, Thom struck up an instant friendship with Colin Greenwood, universally accepted as the most gregarious member of the band. They shared a passion for edgy, dark twisted rock'n'roll - most clearly expressed in their love for Mancunian chroniclers of night-feelings Joy Division and Magazine - and, apparently, a penchant for cross-dressing. The two began to plan the formation of a rock band, with Thom singing, Colin playing bass, and another Abingdon student Ed O'Brien on guitars. Besides sharing similar tastes and temperaments, Thom was most struck by Ed's passing resemblance to Morrissey.

The trio started performing with the accompaniment of a rickety drum-machine, but the appearance of Phil Selway in the ranks added a warm-blooded percussion sensibility to the outfit. Naming themselves On A Friday, in reference to the day they would rehearse, the band performed hesitant shows around Oxford, with Colin's younger brother Jonny accompanying on harmonica.

On A Friday's nascent ascent to superstardom was temporarily halted by the onset of the boys' university careers, sensibly putting dreams of rock action on ice while Thom pursued a degree in Fine Art and Literature at Exeter, Colin reading English at Cambridge, Ed taking Politics at Manchester and Phil at Liverpool. But in downtime, weekends home and holiday periods, the band would reconvene for rehearsals and shows before friends. Some gigs involved brass sections; others a hectic and hurtling cover of Elvis Costello's **Pump It Up**.

The Summer of 1991 found the On A Friday boys freed of their university commitments, and ready to invest all their energies in their music. The unwieldy monicker was ditched in favour of a bandname lifted from a song by their beloved Talking Heads: Radiohead. And while most rock-bands can reel off grimy tales of touring toilet venues in abject obscurity, Radiohead didn't have to wait long for the spiny finger of the music industry to beckon them aboard. Indeed, after their first official show as Radiohead, the quintet - Jonny having ascended from mere mouth-harp blower to full-on keyboardist, guitarist and general multi-instrumentalist - fielded interest from no less than twenty record labels.

They signed to Parlophone, the legendary imprint of EMI Records, and soon found themselves in the recording studio. The first fruits of this working relationship was a four-track EP, **Drill**, that hit the shelves in 1992. If the four tracks contained herein countenanced only the merest glimmers of the majesty Radiohead would soon display, the band were still very green. A bout of touring alongside such artists as Tears For Fears, James and PJ Harvey would solve this and gain the band vital experience, not to mention contact with artists further along in the game.

The band followed **Drill** with their debut album, **Pablo Honey**. Again, it remains an impressive debut, but still just a sketch of the great musical leap

Radiohead would soon be making. However, in the context of the music scene at the time, it sat a satisfying distance apart from its contemporaries.

The year was 1993, and the brutal hegemony the Grunge era had been holding over the world was beginning to break. Sure, Pearl Jam would continue to re-infuse stadium rock with an electrifying and personal intensity (they would become kindred spirits with Radiohead in terms of their integrity and their refusal to bow down to the corporate bullshit that comes with globe-straddling success, even though their music would remain worlds apart), and Nirvana had still yet to deliver their ultimate masterpiece, the brutal and brutalised In Utero album. But, in the UK at least, the slew of American underground rock acts, signed by Johnny Come Lately labels desperate to cash in on the grunge explosion and sluicing every available musical orifice with often half-baked pseudo punk-rock, had eroded patience for this genre of music.

Britain was in the midst of a confused lull. The Madchester baggy scene had all but died out at this point: the Happy Mondays had reduced themselves to drug-addled wrecks, and the acolytes who followed their every move dissipated by the vagaries of fashion, while the Stone Roses were deep in a self-imposed exile which would ultimately undo their band. Similarly, the Thames Valley Scene, uncharitably (but accurately) identified as 'Shoegazing' - floppy fringed, middle-classed student bands, eyes trained on arrays of FX pedals drowning their slight melodies in lakes of noise in a half-hearted attempt to mask the insubstantiality of their fare - had shrivelled up and died.

The next musical movement was a totally reflexive response to this situation. It was Britpop, at this point in time limited to the brash Kinksy affectations of Blur, and the sweeping glam stomp of Suede. The elegance of the genre's early passions and playfulness had yet to fall into stodgy dad-rock reverence and retro pointlessness, the apex of which - Noel Gallagher of Oasis telling an audience, gathered to watch his band at their peak at Knebworth Castle, to worship a videoscreen depicting the long-dead John Lennon - seemed to suggest rock'n'roll utterly dead as an artform that might still have something to say.

Radiohead had little or nothing to do with this movement in the slightest. Sure, there was an errant Englishness to their music, but it owed more to the stadium bombast of U2 and Simple Minds, or the sweeping post-psychedelic sprawl of Pink Floyd, or the sinking, seeping noise-experiments of My Bloody Valentine, than rose-tinted memories of 1960s England. Also, there was a sizeable American influence on the band, not least in their tender anthemicism, seemingly lifted wholesale from the REM guidebook to playing rock'n'roll that aims for the mainstream without sacrificing its soul. And the serrated sense of dynamics that operated as the axle for some of their best early material echoed the similar template rocked by Boston's The Pixies, while the ear-baffling squalls of distortion and feedback that exploded and raged in the background were fallout from the nuclear artpunk of Sonic Youth. This transatlantic sensibility, and desire to charm more than just the first row of the Dublin Castle, would serve the band well, and see them ascend to higher levels of international success than their deathlessly-parochial 'contemporaries' could ever imagine.

Success wouldn't be instant for Radiohead, however. The British music press, which still had some control over the music scene of the time, ignored **Pablo Honey**'s rockin' largesse and sweeping melodics in favour of the glitz and grunge of the period. So the band were shipped over to the states for some hardcore touring, alongside Tears For Fears and Belly. And then something peculiar happened.

The band's first single off **Pablo Honey** exploded in America, becoming a massive radio-hit and earning coveted Heavy Rotation on MTV that Summer. **Creep** was a deceptively simple song, built on the Pixies' hitherto-noted quiet-loud dynamic, a killer little trick that nevertheless was murderously effective. Add to that a sense of soured melodicism which nodded towards the pained likes of prime REM, and a shredded, blood-splattered explosion of distorted guitar that echoed throughout, lifted wholesale from Nirvana's punishing howls of angst, and it's no surprise these British boys were soon the taste of the States, their noise translating very smoothly to an America still very much in the grip of the grunge revolution.

Creep opens with a tender music-box melody, as Yorke relates his tale of disaffection, listing a paean to his object of desire, all the time using the language of the displaced; this is the poetry more of a stalker than a lover, the girl(?) in question placed upon a pedestal and used more as an indicator of how removed from society the narrator is, rather than as an object for tenderness or true love.

"I wish I was special," Yorke murmurs, as a crunch of guitar is discharged in the foreground, almost by accident.

"You're so fucking special," he sings again, as the guitar grates two more times, with an intense, foreboding fervour.

"But I'm a creep," Yorke contends, as the guitars burn into an acrid wave of tremelo-treated noise, mimicking the earlier music-box tune but with about seventeen-trillion decibels of psychedelic sonic muscle added for good measure. With it's moving middle-eight, Yorke poignantly howling and singing like a fallen angel over the apocalyptic guitar whiteout, the song was a work of genius, four minutes or so of goosepimple-inducing guitar-pop that worked as an example of traditional songwriting, while simultaneously monkeying about with all the formulas, with electrifying results.

Creep was, unsurprisingly, Pablo Honey's absolute standout track, but there were other fine moments on the album. There was the squalling noise-out of Vegetable, the closing wind-down of Blow Out. And there was, of course, the insouciant Anyone Can Play Guitar, the tune which seemed to most rile the music press of the time (well, at least it got their attention). Opening with phased guitar dissonance, it unfurled into a churning spiteful attack on dullard indie-rock's fearful lack of ambition, the star here the twisted guitar jags and Yorke's swelling vocals.

But, for a time at least, Radiohead would navigate their punishing international touring and press commitments known only as 'The Creep band'... The experience would engender an enduring and deserved distrust of the music press, and the machinations of a record industry built to chew up and spit out one-hit wonders. It would sire projects like Meeting People Is Easy, the dispiriting treatise on the band's enduring sense of displacement while on the road which was released on video at the end of the 90s. It would also compel the band to create a follow-up which would stomp the memory of that song defiantly into the dust.

You could say they succeeded.

The Bends, then. If ever there was a record which confirmed its creators more than the one-hit-wonders they might've been acclaimed as, this was it. A dense fog of ennui, angst and progressive, highly textured art-rock which flirted gamely with self-indulgence while never tumbling over that particular precipice, this was the album where Radiohead began exploring the grey area between erudite stadium rock and inward-looking experimental explorations.

There was an impressive team manning the mixing desk for the album. John Leckie, famed for his work with The Stone Roses and a veteran of many similarly stellar production assignments, was the producer. Mixing was shared between Leckie, Radiohead, and the duo of Sean Slade & Paul Q Kolderie, who'd helmed Pablo Honey, and whose gift for warm sonic tones had pretty much shaped the welcoming flannel-clad jangle of American indie-rock throughout the late 80s/early 90s. Meanwhile, the gilded psychedelic jangle of Black Star was produced by Radiohead themselves, with assistance from Leckie and a young gentleman named Nigel Godrich who would soon become an integral part of Radiohead's studio ensemble in years to come.

But it was Leckie's expertise and experience in the studio which drew from Radiohead such a focused and clear performance of this new material. The fuzzy shamble that afflicted some part of Pablo Honey was absent. In its place lay a sense of vision and purpose, a shaking free of the indie-rock dust that had previously afflicted their music. Coursing through The Bends' veins were spores of space-rock dreaminess, near-complex near-prog arrangements, and a newfound emotional depth to Yorke's vocal, no longer content to express only the snottiest or bleakest of emotional fits and starts: the whole gamut of life's experiences, from ecstasy to agony, began to reverberate through the long, sometimes wordless sighs and howls he laced the album with.

One influence Yorke felt no shame in wearing upon his sleeve was Jeff Buckley. Though at this point still something of a cult concern – despite being praised to the high heavens by the more open-minded critical cognoscenti - Yorke openly confessed that Buckley's languid, uninhibited and emotive vocal gymnastics, as featured on 1994's Grace debut album (never self-indulgent, never histrionic, always beautiful and moving) forced him to raise his game, re-assess how he approached his vocal performances.

Nowhere is this more apparent that on Fake Plastic Trees. A beautiful, meditative, slow-burning track, it set the framework for The Bends' finest moments. It was, in essence, melodically simple and sparse, the band shading in the finer details - acoustic strum blazing into tremelo-heavy squall, church organs and strings sighing in the distance with a subtlety beyond all the Britpop dullards who went running to orchestras when their glum balladry failed to scrape the emotional peaks and troughs - to build something that was complex and endlessly fascinating, and instantly and consistently moving.

But the star, of course, is Yorke's vocal. Keening, gentle, fragile, it opens the song with a folky intimacy, recalling, say, Nick Drake or John Martyn. Then, as the song progresses, it swells and dissipates like a breeze throughout, sometimes a shadow of a whisper, sometimes a gorgeous siren call reverberating through the sonics, always potent and poignant. The final passage, Yorke singing "If I could be who you wanted," his words so brittle the slightest noise could shatter them, is heart-breaking.

Meanwhile, the allusions and metaphysics of the imagery contained in **Fake Plastic Trees** indicated a growing lower-p politicism brewing within the band. The back sleeve of **Pablo Honey** had deconstructed the barcode format, symbolising the band's refusal to fit comfortably within the corporate format. Now, they're tempering a sweet ballad with imagery of the fallibilty and ultimate pointlessness of modern life, not just declaring it 'Rubbish' like Blur had in 1993, but picking apart sad and hilarious images like that of a plastic surgeon in the 80s forever defeated by gravity.

This sensibility swells behind the closing track, **Street Spirit (Fade Out)**. As the title suggests, at heart this song tells of the human spirit often disregarded by urban machinations, though to describe it thusly in such clumsy Wolfie Smith-type rhetoric is to do an injustice to such a moving and subtle song. No, **Street Spirit** is a hymn to the hum of human life constrained by an ever-colder society, a sombre guitar line circling round and round as Yorke sings of the "Rows of houses all bearing down on me," his voice breaking as he sings "Fade out again," giving himself over to the inevitable. Downbeat yes, but strangely stirring too - cathartic and expressive. And again, it's a masterpiece of simplicity, all the power contained in the rolling guitar line, ghostly synths, shimmering drums and Yorke's vocal.

Not all of the songs on **The Bends** drew from this well of restrained elegance, measured power. There was **Just**, a churning, queasy epic of squalling psychedelia. The chorus was key, Yorke repeating "You do it to yourself, you do, and that's what really hurts," over cyclic riffs, until the guitars and synths all lock into the uneasy ascending central riff of the song, a stomping spiny beast torn from the grooves of an early Sabbath album and then enrolled in prog finishing school to deliver a rockout that's all clammy and sinister and smart at once.

Treated guitar and a sweet and edgy psychedelic guitar figure characterised **My Iron Lung**, Yorke's voice sultry and languid where it had previously been chaste or chastened. On this track, it's a thing to luxuriate in, savouring every sharp, caustic, cynical observation on a vacant generation, until the needling bass throb explodes into a Nirvana-esque thrashout halfway through. That said raucous segue soon bleeds back into acrid/placid psychedelia is only further proof of Radiohead's poise and power.

But it was Radiohead's blend of a fragile folky simplicity, bolstered by their gift for deft musical complexity that made **The Bends** such a huge success (not to mention, of course, Yorke's lucid examinations of a very 21st Century psychosis, a sense of constant and total displacement, an angst born of disgust with the world surrounding him). Nowhere was this best evinced that on **High & Dry**, where Phil Selway's loose breakbeat is topped with even looser, graceful acoustic guitars. The joy here is in the ease of Yorke's vocal, slight and slim but liquid and lashing about every note with an almost lazy calm. The way he slips into an unhurried falsetto on the chorus, "Don't leave me high / Don't leave me dry") is utterly, utterly charming.

The Bends surely and inarguably placed Radiohead at the vanguard of the brave and incisive creative forces in rock'n'roll. No longer were they the U2 stadium rock-wannabes they'd been derided as in the press - they'd scooped that very stadia success without tampering with their formula; indeed, if anything, making it all the more 'difficult' and idiosyncratic. And no longer were they one-hit-wonders. No, now they had a genuine modern-classic of an album behind them. Now the press which had chided them previously breathed down their neck, impatiently, hungrily waiting to see what their next step would be. How on earth could they ever follow **The Bends**?

By bettering it. By widening their scope, expanding the complexity, exploring further the electroid landscapes and twists that shaded elements of **The Bends**. By tapping deeper and harder into the hyper-modern sense of anxiety which had powered **The Bends**' finer tracks, by letting the band's sharp musicianship and Yorke's lyrical vocal style take free reign. "I'm amazed that I survived," he sings in **Airbag**. But **OK Computer** wasn't a mere survival of the rush of fame and acclaim that had greeted the band since **Creep** and **The Bends**. It was a mantra for a whole series of steps further onward.

The first hints of what Radiohead were brewing in the studio with Nigel Godrich surfaced in late 1995, with the release of **Help**, a charity record assembled to aid the children suffering in war-torn Bosnia. Adhering to John

Lennon's observation that records should be like newspapers, a commandment he himself put into practise with his **Instant Karma** single, recorded on a monday and released the following friday, recording sessions for the album were held on Sunday September 3rd, 1995, as 18 artists - including Blur, Noel Gallagher and Paul Weller - each recorded and mixed a track, under the proviso that it couldn't extend longer than 3 minutes and 45 seconds.

Radiohead delivered **Lucky**, which would later form one of the many highlights of **OK Computer**. A slow brooding melody is topped off with a similarly slow, brooding vocal from Yorke, singing of death and destruction and hubris and decay, echoing the bleak sentiments of The Specials' brilliant second album, 1980's **More Specials** (especially songs like **Stereotypes Pts 1 & 2** and **International Jetset**) while never actually sounding like them. Then, as Yorke croons, "Pull me out of the aircrash", just about the most beautiful, liquid guitar break soars from amongst the humming synths and whirling oscillators. The guitar work on **OK Computer**, all treated with electronics and fed through processors and FX pedals until they barely resembled traditional instruments, most surely marked the band's debt to prog-rock, from gargantuan, planet-straddling acts like Pink Floyd, through to more esoteric and leftfield influences like King Crimson and Van Der Graaf Generator.

That **OK Computer** would drag these bizarre musical oddities into the mainstream is further testament to Radiohead's gift.

Vague ghosts of the electronica which would rule Radiohead's subsequent two albums surfaced in **OK Computer**'s opening track, **Airbag**. Selway's stop-start drumbreak is fed through various sonic filters until it closer resembles a drum-machine than an acoustic kit, fidgeting and fibrillating behind the austere sweep of the music. And Yorke's vocal indicates just how comfortable he is with his own style now, as he wraps the words into flows of melody and sighing, wordless screes, at times as much an instrument as the guitars and the synths. Brilliantly, the song breaks down about three minutes in, only for pulsing, treated drum samples to kick in with a most fecund, murky funk, restarting the song for one last giddy run-through, again anticipating the workouts of **Kid A** and **Amnesiac**.

On **OK Computer**, **Airbag** segues seamlessly into **Paranoid Android**, the seemingly-suicidal choice for first single off the album. Of course, such a judgement doesn't anticipate the strength of Radiohead's fanbase at this point, who had no problem with sending such an unwieldy, radio-unfriendly slab of experimentation into the upper reaches of the charts. A jagged, ugly fusion of nursery rhyme and full-on prog-metal rifferama, the six-minutes-plus track has ended up being something of a **Bohemian Rhapsody** for its generation. Though as a song in of itself, the frankenstein lurch from foreboding choral whispers to mogadon thrashout don't gel together like they should - all you can see is the join, not the grand vision - as a statement of Radiohead's refusal to play the game it worked perfectly, and its mixture of grave anti-societal poetics and victimised posturing made for a potent lyrical content.

But the other two singles off **OK Computer** were certainly more traditional, and more successful/less tantrum-esque statements of what the band could do. **Karma Police** was a palatable slab of AOR, underpinned by Yorke's morbid, twisted lyrical games, and sent soaring into the stratosphere by his freeform vocal, loosely playing with the melodies and words and seeming to have a life of its own, free of the song. Then there were the bizarre sampled choral sighs, and the bursts of computer-generated schism bubbling throughout. A trojan horse of complexity, then.

But **No Surprises** was just gorgeous. Another music box melody, this time unsullied by crashing deisel guitar, it was eked out on guitars and xylophone, the see-saw chiming tune caressed by a vocal from Yorke that seemed to steal liberally from the velvet grandeur of Scott Walker, while retaining an opiated wastedness. "No alarms, and no surprises," he sings, almost slurring the last word, the sense of resignation potent, poignant, beautiful.

OK Computer was universally lauded as the masterpiece it was, and the live shows which followed cemented Radiohead's reputation as boundary-obliterating stadium-rock gods for a generation too sophisticated for Bono's one-dimensional posturing. The band swiftly sundered all unnecessary contact with the music press that had treated them disrespectfully throughout most of their career. In many ways this was an act of wilful self-possession, as they had proved they no longer the music press for their success, just as they had proved their uncompromising music could carve a new dimension of success for themselves.

But similarly it might've been endemic of the pressure the band had placed themselves under, following the acclaim and success of **OK Computer**. They'd faced the challenge of following up **The Bends** by surpassing expectations. In recording the sequels to **OK Computer**, they would *confound* those very same expectations.

What followed was a pair of albums, recorded simultaneously, that forcefully shifted peoples' perceptions of exactly who and what Radiohead were. Drawing their influences from avant-garde abstract electronica artists like Four Tet and artists from labels like warp (home to the likes of Aphex Twin), Radiohead proceeded to artfully obscure the simplicity of their essential songwriting gift with all manner of post-production playfulness and whimsy.

While many suggested these albums were a surprising step into the leftfield for Radiohead, the processes which led to the remarkable albums **Kid A** and **Amnesiac** weren't that far removed from the way songs on previous albums

had developed. Only, instead of fractured guitar and prog-synth squalling and contorting what were, at heart, fairly simple songs, computer technology and sampling stepped in and pulled the source material into strange and wonderful shapes.

Kid A opened with the wonderfully foreboding Everything In Its Right Place. Yorke's vocal courses edgily over warm but uneasy rhodes keyboard lines, twisted and oversampled and chopped into pieces, until several disembodied and contorted Thom Yorke's are murmuring the song title over and over again. A powerful song, it works subtly and imperceptibly, setting the pace for an album which would move in unexpected ways.

What followed included jazz-influenced instrumentals, washes of electronic abstraction, stirring moments of oddity and brilliance. And, in Optimistic, Radiohead delivered perhaps their most conventional song of the set. Over rumbling drums and bruised guitars ringing out from the detuned New York Sonic Youth chronicled, Thom Yorke crooned not-entirely-uncynically of "Trying the best you can," as the clouds of disquiet gathered grim and grey at the edges. The segue of this track, into the following eddy and flow of In Limbo, was particularly exquisite.

Less than a year later, Kid A's companion piece Amnesiac surfaced. Originally pitched by the label as the more guitar-friendly yang to Kid A's electroid ying, presumably by way of a sop to the Radiohead fans who would feel alienated by the oddity of their latest generical shift, it was nothing of the sort. For one thing, Kid A blended its newfound influences with a subtlety which meant it was no gaudy leap into the unknown. Fresh, yes. Unexpected, undoubtedly. But always Radiohead.

And Amnesiac was certainly no step backwards. It shared its immediate predecessor's predeliction for shifting the band into unfamiliar territory, following that impulse through with no quarter asked or given. The first single, Pyramid Song was a haunting, piano-led piece. Quite, quite beautiful, it owed perhaps more to the jazzed-out folk-prog of 70s-era John Martyn than any post-sampler, computer aided 'tronica. As ever, the joy lies in Yorke's vocal, and Amnesiac gives plenty of opportunities to savour how it has matured, wavering by choice, weighed heavy with experience and a deeper sense of the emotions only he can deliver. Again, his keening vocals are used as an instrument on this song, as the strings ape and fly in parallel to his voice. The result is an uneasy, powerful slice of unpretentious, jazz-influenced alt-pop.

Knives Out had been a live favourite of the band's for some time, and it's place in Amnesiac has often been suggested as incongruous. And, sure, its guitar-led dark, shadowy melodicism might seem out of place in terms of the more futuristic experiments on the album. But, firstly, listen to the gentle shades of echo tracing Yorke's vocal and answer whether the band might've used such a trick before the maelstrom of unfamiliar techniques explored on these two albums.

Then listen to the albums together as a whole, and get a sense of what Radiohead have achieved here. Both albums were huge successes, especially in the USA, where the band's leftfield and avant garde influences flew even further beneath the radar than at home. Once again, the band's refusal to ape the slim pickings offered by the mainstream resulted in the mainstream following their singular path instead. And, once again, Radiohead have raised people's expectations for whatever will follow under the band's aegis. The only difference this time is that no-one can exactly predict where their errant muses will take them this time.

All that's for sure is that they'll be worth following.

Stevie Chick has been a freelance music writer for four years, contributing to Melody Maker, NME, Kerrang!, The Times, the Evening Standard and Sleaze Nation, and is currently a contributing editor of Careless Talk Costs Lives. He lives in London and has recently completed work on his book Don't Stop Now: The Ballad Of Guided By Voices, the amazing tale of 30-something songwriter Robert Pollard's ascent from school teacher obscurity to indie-rock superstardom.

Discography:Albums

Pablo Honey

You
Creep
How Do You?
Stop Whispering
Thinking About You
Anyone Can Play Guitar
Ripcord
Vegetable
Prove Yourself
I Can't
Lurgee
Blow Out

Release Date: February 1993
Highest Chart Position: 22
Weeks On Chart: 82

The Bends

Planet Telex
The Bends
High & Dry
Fake Plastic Trees
Bones
Nice Dream
Just
My Iron Lung
Bulletproof.. I wish I was
Black Star
Sulk
Street Spirit (fade out)

Release Date: March 1995
Highest Chart Position: 4
Weeks On Chart: 160

OK Computer

Airbag
Paranoid Android
Subterranean Homesick Alien
Exit Music (for a film)
Let Down
Karma Police
Fitter Happier
Electioneering
Climbing up the Walls
No Surprises
Lucky
The Tourist

Release Date: June 1997
Highest Chart Position: 1
Weeks On Chart: 73

Kid A

Everything In Its Right Place
Kid A
The National Anthem
How To Disappear Completely
Treefingers
Optimistic
In Limbo
Idioteque
Morning Bell
Motion Picture Soundtrack

Release Date: October 2000
Highest Chart Position: 1
Weeks On Chart: 15

Amnesiac

Packt Like Sardines In A Crushd Tin Box
Pyramid Song
Pulk/Pull Revolving Doors
You And Whose Army?
I Might Be Wrong
Knives Out
Morning Bell / Amnesiac
Dollars And Cents
Hunting Bears
Like Spinning Plates
Life In A Glass Jar

Release Date: June 2001
Highest Chart Position: 1
Weeks On Chart: 12

I Might Be Wrong – Live Recordings

The National Anthem (live)
I Might Be Wrong (live)
Morning Bell (live)
Like Spinning Plates (live)
Idioteque (live)
Everything In Its Right Place (live)
Dollars And Cents (live)
True Love Waits (live)

Release Date: October 2001
Not chart eligible

Discography:Singles

Drill EP
b/w *Prove Yourself, Stupid Car, You, Thinking About You*
Release Date: May 1992
Highest Chart Position: n/a
Weeks On Chart: n/a

Creep
b/w *Lurgee, Inside My Head, Million $ Question*
Release Date: September 1992,
Highest Chart Position: 78
Weeks On Chart: 1

Anyone Can Play Guitar
b/w *Faithless The Wonder Boy, Coke Babies*
Release Date: February 1993
Highest Chart Position: 32
Weeks On Chart: 2

Pop Is Dead
b/w *Banana Co.* (acoustic), *Creep* (live), *Ripcord* (live)
Release Date: May 1993
Highest Chart Position: 42
Weeks On Chart: 2

Creep
CD: b/w *Yes I Am, Blow Out* (remix), *Inside My Head* (live at the Metro)
12": b/w *Creep* (acoustic version from K-ROQ radio session in USA),
You (live at the Metro), *Vegetable* (live at the Metro),
Killer Cars (live at the Metro)
Release Date: September 1993
Highest Chart Position: 7
Weeks On Chart: 6

My Iron Lung
CD1: b/w *Punchdrunk Lovesick Singalong, Lozenge Of Love*
CD2: b/w *Lewis (mistreated), Permanent Daylight, You Never Wash
Up After Yourself*
12": b/w *Punchdrunk Lovesick Singalong, The Trickster,
Lewis (mistreated)*
Release Date: September 1994
Highest Chart Position: 24
Weeks On Chart: 2

High & Dry/Planet Telex
CD1: b/w *Maquiladora, Planet Telex* (hexidecimal mix)
CD2: b/w *Killer Cars, Planet Telex* (LFO JD mix)
12": b/w *Planet Telex* (hexidecimal mix), *Planet Telex* (LFO JD mix),
Planet Telex (hexideximal dub mix)
Release Date: February 1995
Highest Chart Position: 17
Weeks On Chart: 4

Fake Plastic Trees
CD1: b/w *India Rubber, How Can You Be Sure?*
CD2: b/w *Fake Plastic Trees* (acoustic, live in London), *Bullet Proof... I
Wish I Was* (acoustic, live in London), *Street Spirit* (acoustic, live in
London)
Release Date: May 1995
Highest Chart Position: 20
Weeks On Chart: 4

Just
CD1: b/w *Planet Telex* (Karma Sunra mix), *Killer Cars* (Modagon version)
CD2: b/w *Bones* (live), *Planet Telex* (live), *Anyone Can Play Guitar* (live)
Release Date: August 1995
Highest Chart Position: 19
Weeks On Chart: 3

Street Spirit (Fade Out)
CD1: b/w *Talkshow Host, Bishop's Robes*
CD2: b/w *Banana Co, Molasses*
Release Date: January 1996
Highest Chart Position: 5
Weeks On Chart: 4

Paranoid Android
CD1: b/w *Polyethylene (parts 1 & 2),Pearly**
CD2: b/w *A Reminder, Melatonin*
Release Date: 1997
Highest Chart Position: 3
Weeks On Chart: 5

Karma Police
CD1: b/w *Meeting In The Aisle, Lull*
CD2: b/w *Climbing Up The Walls* (zero 7 mix),
Climbing Up The Walls (fila brazilia mix)
Release Date: 1997
Highest Chart Position: 8
Weeks On Chart: 4

No Surprises
CD1: b/w *Palo Alto, How I Made My Millions*
CD2: b/w *Airbag* (live - Berlin, 3-Nov-97),
Lucky (live - Florence, 30-Oct-97)
Release Date: January 1998
Highest Chart Position: 4
Weeks On Chart: 7

Pyramid Song
CD1: *The Amazing Sounds Of Orgy, Trans-atlantic Drawl*
CD2: *Fast-track, Kinetic*
Release Date: May 2001
Highest Chart Position: 5
Weeks On Chart: 2

Knives Out
CD1: b/w *Cuttooth, Life In A Glass House* [full length version]
CD2: b/w *Worrywort, Fog*
Release Date: August 2001
Highest Chart Position: 13
Weeks On Chart: 5

GUITAR TAB GLOSSARY**

TABLATURE EXPLANATION

READING TABLATURE: Tablature illustrates the six strings of the guitar. Notes and chords are indicated by the placement of fret numbers on a given string(s).

String ⑥ **3rd** *Fret*   *String* ① **12th** *Fret*   A "C" Chord   "C" Chord Arpeggiated
String ③ **13th** *Fret*

BENDING NOTES

HALF STEP: Play the note and bend string one half step.*

WHOLE STEP: Play the note and bend string one whole step.

WHOLE STEP AND A HALF: Play the note and bend string a whole step and a half.

QUARTER-TONE BEND: Play the note and bend string slightly to the equivalent of half a fret.

PREBEND (Ghost Bend): Bend to the specified note, before the string is picked.

PREBEND AND RELEASE: Bend the string, play it, then release to the original note.

REVERSE BEND: Play the already-bent string, then immediately drop it down to the fretted note.

BEND AND RELEASE: Play the note and gradually bend to the next pitch, then release to the original note. Only the first note is attacked.

*A half step is the smallest interval in Western music; it is equal to one fret. A whole step equals two frets.

UNISON BEND: Play both notes and immediately bend the lower note to the same pitch as the higher note.

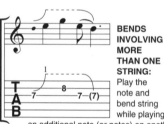

DOUBLE NOTE BEND: Play both notes and immediately bend both strings simultaneously.

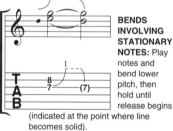

BENDS INVOLVING MORE THAN ONE STRING: Play the note and bend string while playing an additional note (or notes) on another string(s). Upon release, relieve pressure from additional note(s), causing original note to sound alone.

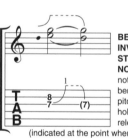

BENDS INVOLVING STATIONARY NOTES: Play notes and bend lower pitch, then hold until release begins (indicated at the point where line becomes solid).

TREMOLO BAR

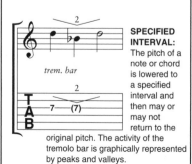

trem. bar

SPECIFIED INTERVAL: The pitch of a note or chord is lowered to a specified interval and then may or may not return to the original pitch. The activity of the tremolo bar is graphically represented by peaks and valleys.

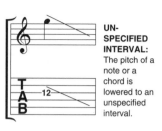

UN-SPECIFIED INTERVAL: The pitch of a note or a chord is lowered to an unspecified interval.

HARMONICS

harm.   harm. (8va)

harm.   harm.

NATURAL HARMONIC: A finger of the fret hand lightly touches the note or notes indicated in the tab and is played by the pick hand.

A.H.

ARTIFICIAL HARMONIC: The first tab number is fretted, then the pick hand produces the harmonic by using a finger to lightly touch the same string at the second tab number (in parenthesis) and is then picked by another finger.

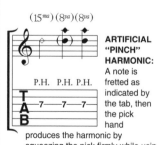

ARTIFICIAL "PINCH" HARMONIC: A note is fretted as indicated by the tab, then the pick hand produces the harmonic by squeezing the pick firmly while using the tip of the index finger in the pick attack. If parenthesis are found around the fretted note, it does not sound. No parenthesis means both the fretted note and A.H. are heard simultaneously.

**By Kenn Chipkin and Aaron Stang

RHYTHM SLASHES

STRUM INDICATIONS: Strum with indicated rhythm.

The chord voicings are found on the first page of the transcription underneath the song title.

SINGLE NOTES IN SLASH NOTATION: A regular notehead indicates a single note. The circled number below the note indicates which string of the chord to strike. If the note is not in the chord, the fret number will be indicated above the note(s).

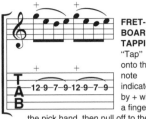

FRET-BOARD TAPPING: "Tap" onto the note indicated by + with a finger of the pick hand, then pull off to the following note held by the fret hand.

TAP SLIDE: Same as fretboard tapping, but the tapped note is slid randomly up the fretboard, then pulled off to the following note.

SHORT GLISSAN-DO: Play note for its full value and slide in specified direction at the last possible moment.

PICK SLIDE: Slide the edge of the pick in specified direction across the length of the string(s).

TRILL: Hammer on and pull off consecutively and as fast as possible between the original note and the grace note.

ACCENT: Notes or chords are to be played with added emphasis.

ARTICULATIONS

HAMMER ON: Play lower note, then "hammer on" to higher note with another finger. Only the first note is attacked.

LEFT HAND HAMMER: Hammer on the first note played on each string with the left hand.

PULL OFF: Play higher note, then "pull off" to lower note with another finger. Only the first note is attacked.

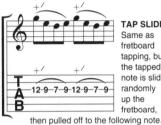

BEND AND TAP TECHNIQUE: Play note and bend to specified interval. While holding bend, tap onto note indicated.

LEGATO SLIDE: Play note and slide to the following note. (Only first note is attacked).

LONG GLISSAN-DO: Play note and slide in specified direction for the full value of the note.

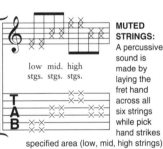

low mid. high
stgs. stgs. stgs.

MUTED STRINGS: A percussive sound is made by laying the fret hand across all six strings while pick hand strikes specified area (low, mid, high strings).

P.M.

PALM MUTE: The note or notes are muted by the palm of the pick hand by lightly touching the string(s) near the bridge.

trem. pick

TREMOLO PICKING: The note or notes are picked as fast as possible.

STACCATO (Detached Notes): Notes or chords are to be played roughly half their actual value and with separation.

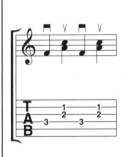

DOWN STROKES AND UPSTROKES: Notes or chords are to be played with either a downstroke (■) or upstroke (v) of the pick.

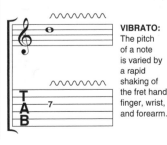

VIBRATO: The pitch of a note is varied by a rapid shaking of the fret hand finger, wrist, and forearm.

Airbag

Words and Music by
THOMAS YORKE, COLIN GREENWOOD, EDWARD O'BRIEN,
PHILIP SELWAY AND JONATHAN GREENWOOD

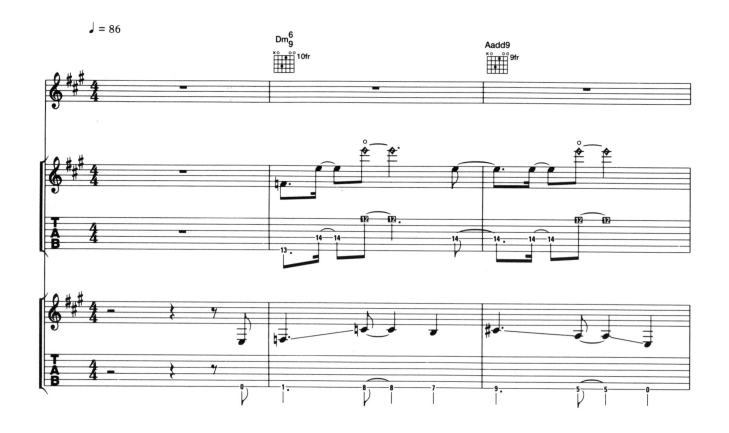

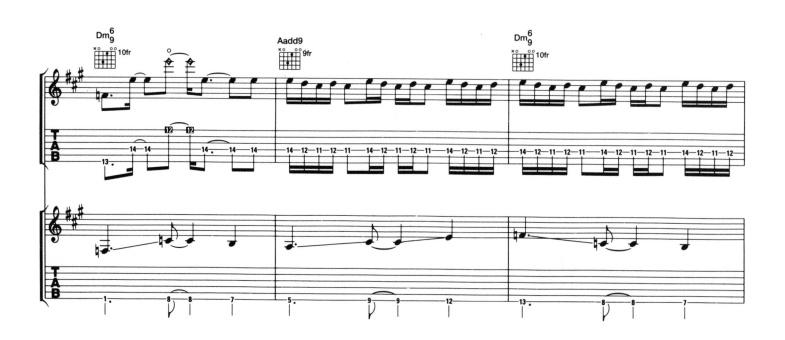

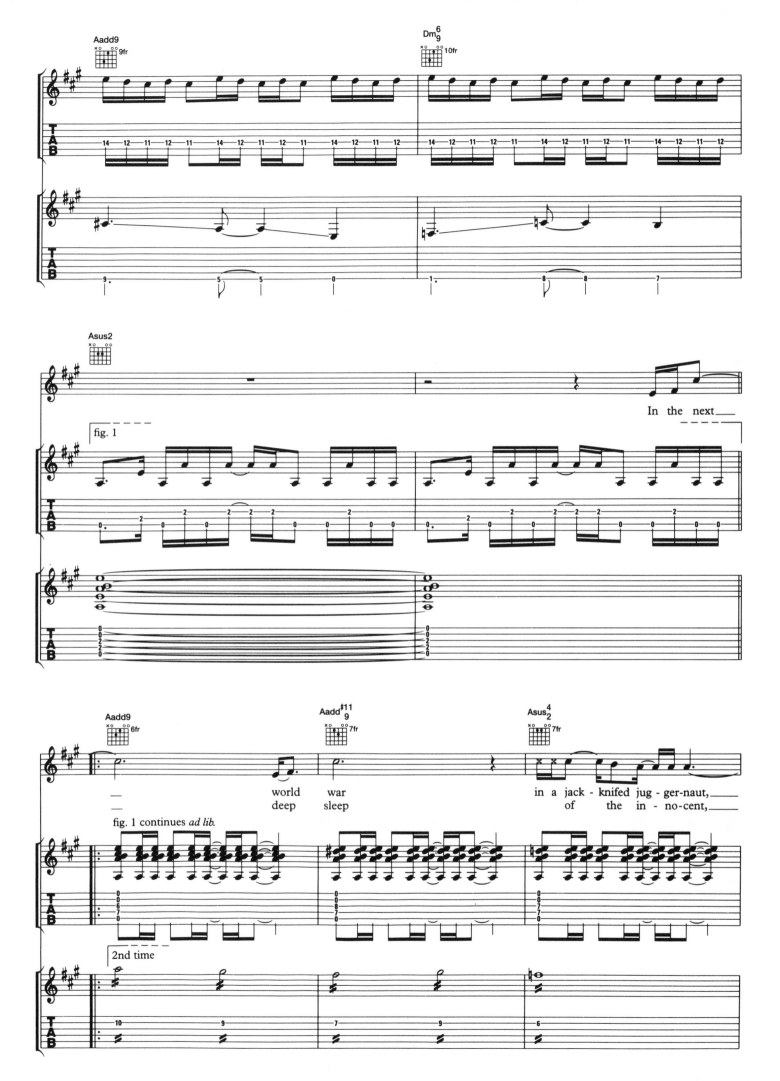

In the next____

world war   deep sleep
deep sleep

in a jack-knifed jug-ger-naut,____
of   the   in-no-cent,____

fig. 1 continues *ad lib.*

2nd time

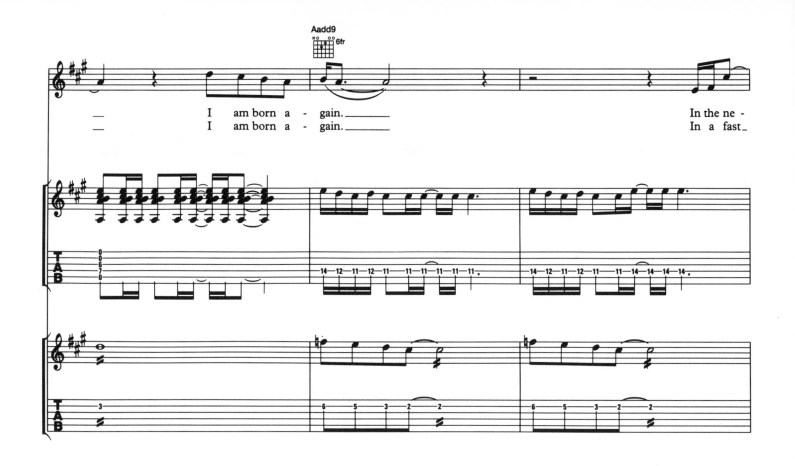

I am born a - gain. _____

I am born a - gain. _____

In the ne -

In a fast_

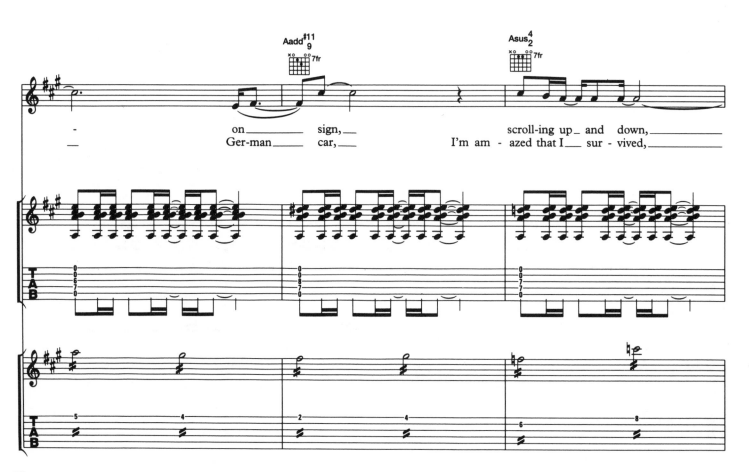

- on _____ sign, _____

Ger-man _____ car, _____

scroll-ing up_ and down, _____

I'm am - azed that I_ sur - vived, _____

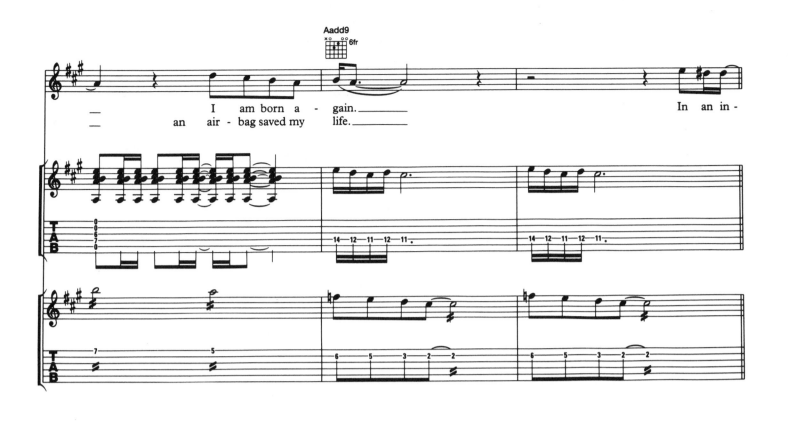

I am born a - gain._____ In an in-
an air - bag saved my life._____

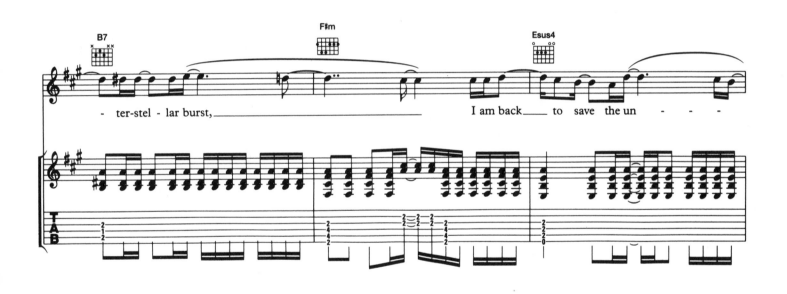

- ter-stel - lar burst,_____ I am back___ to save the un - - -

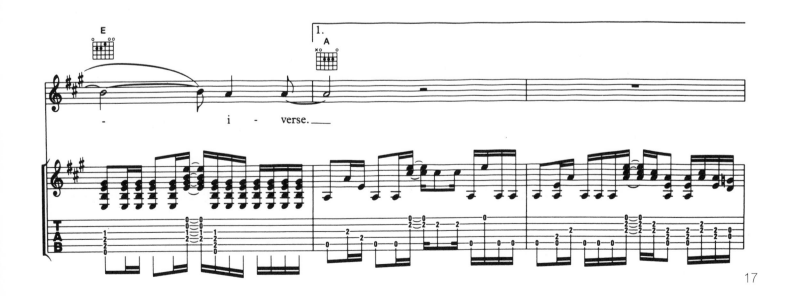

- i - verse.___

In a deep____

doubled *ad lib.* with slide guitar

In an in - ter-stel - lar burst,_____

I am back____ to save the un - - - - i - verse.

In an in - ter-stel - lar burst,_____

I am back____ to save the un - - - - i - verse.

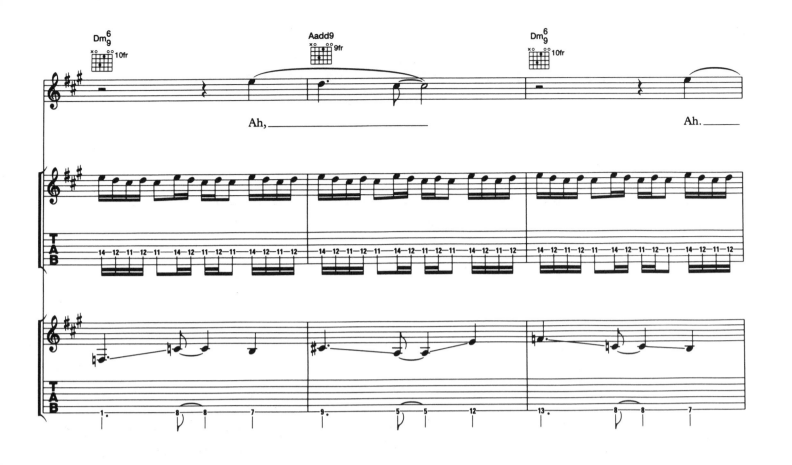

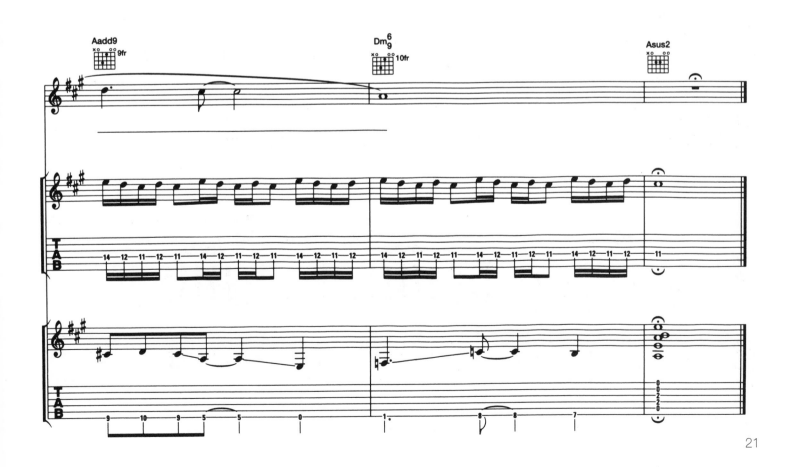

Anyone Can Play Guitar

Words and Music by
THOMAS YORKE, EDWARD O'BRIEN, COLIN GREENWOOD,
JONATHAN GREENWOOD and PHILIP SELWAY

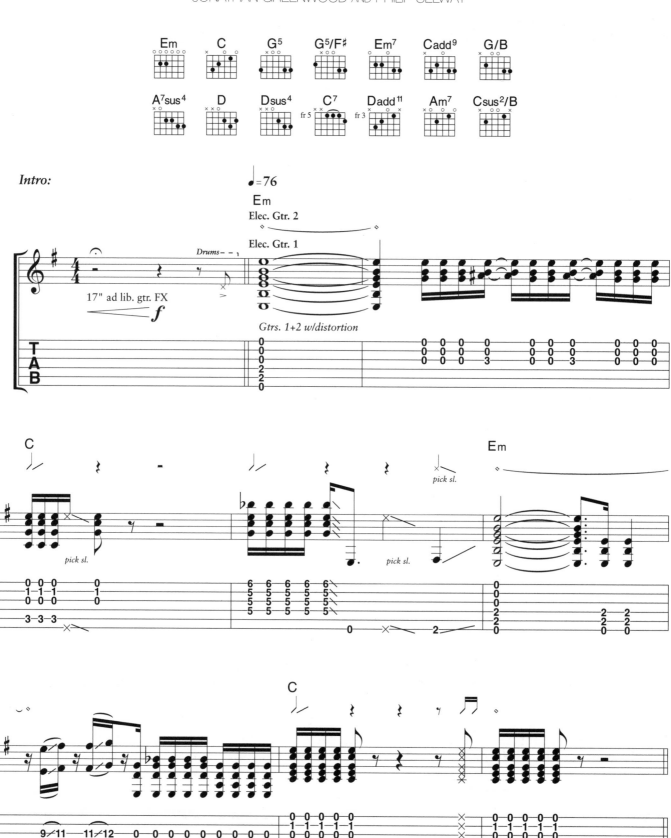

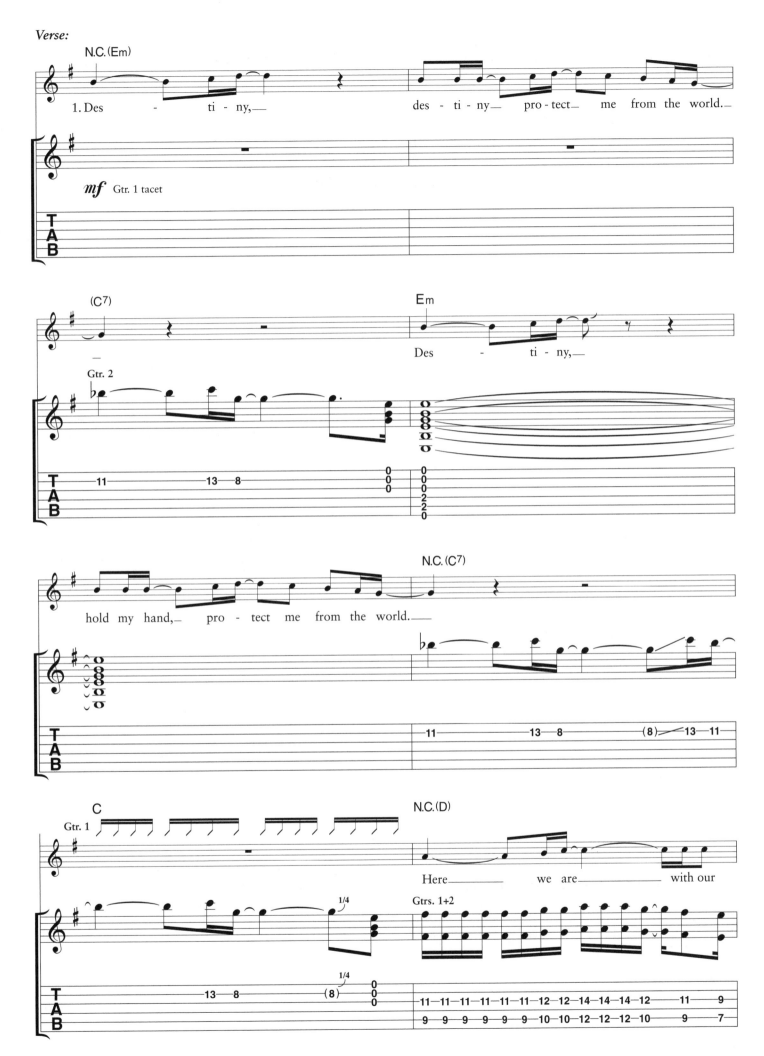

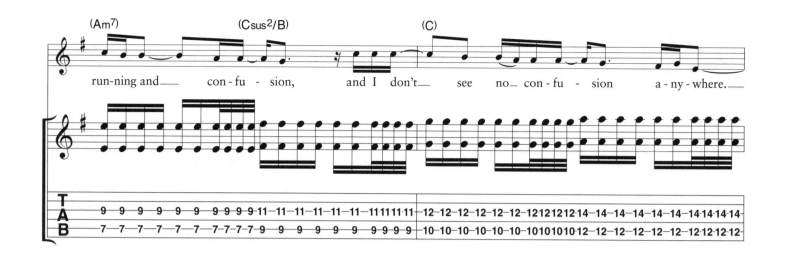

run-ning and___ con-fu-sion, and I don't___ see no___ con-fu-sion a-ny-where.___

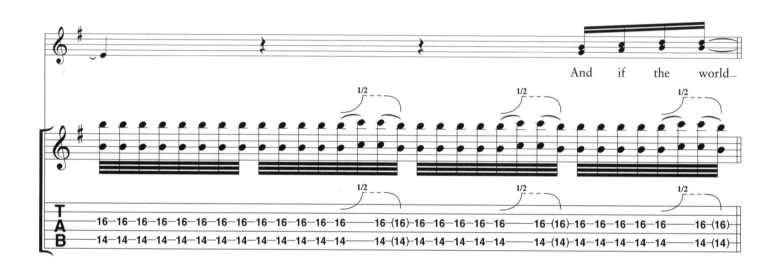

And if the world___

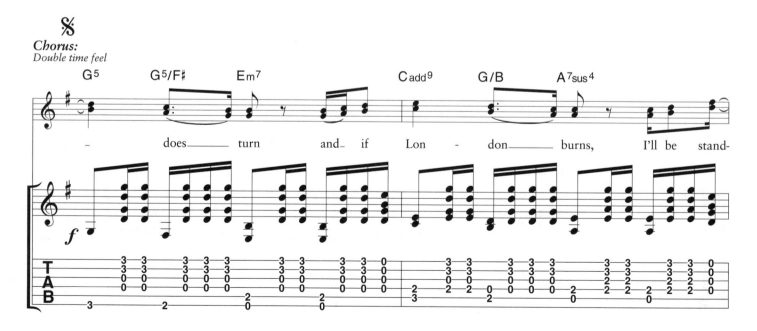

Chorus:
Double time feel

___ does___ turn and___ if Lon - don___ burns, I'll be stand-

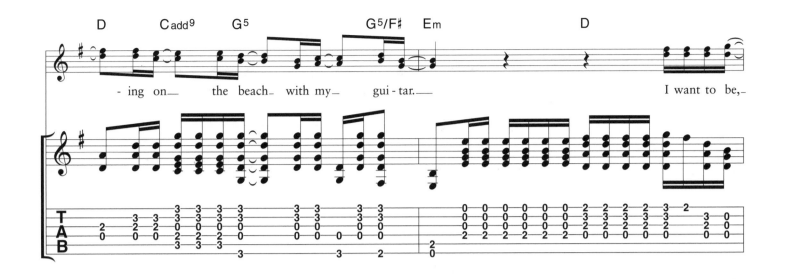

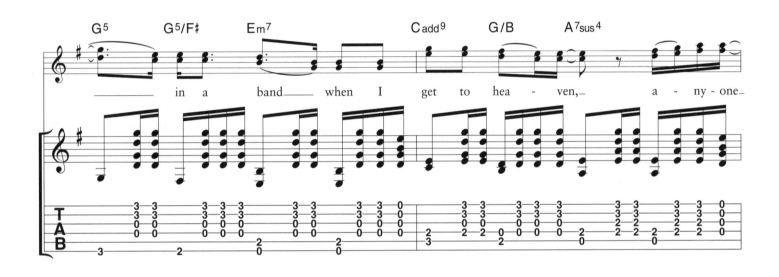

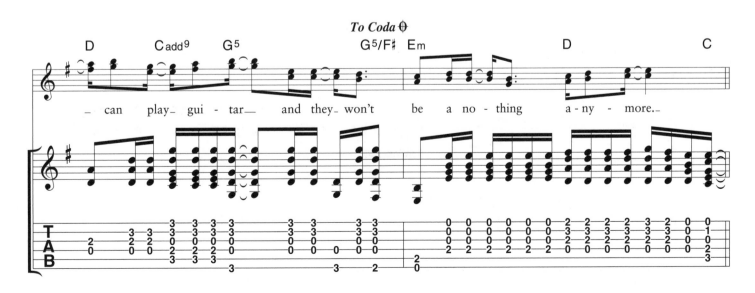

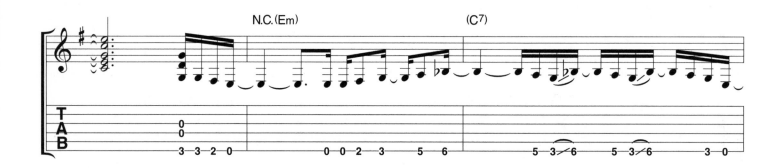

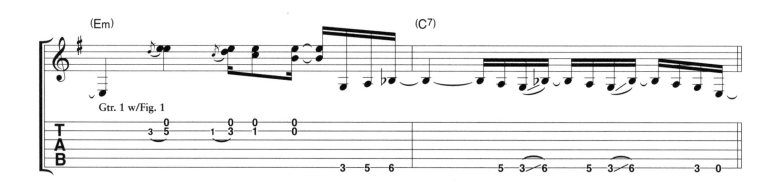

Verse:

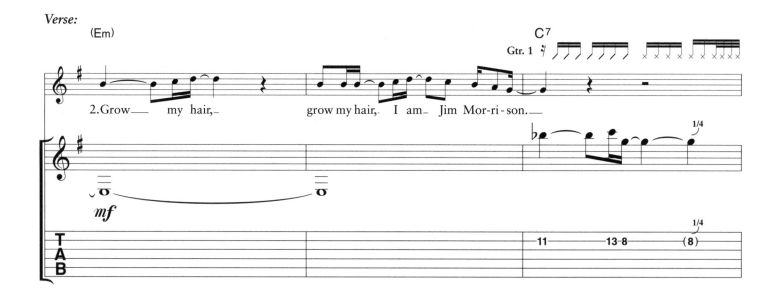

2.Grow___ my hair,___ grow my hair, I am___ Jim Mor-ri-son.___

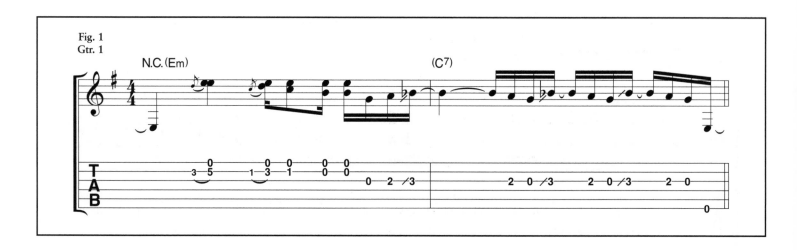

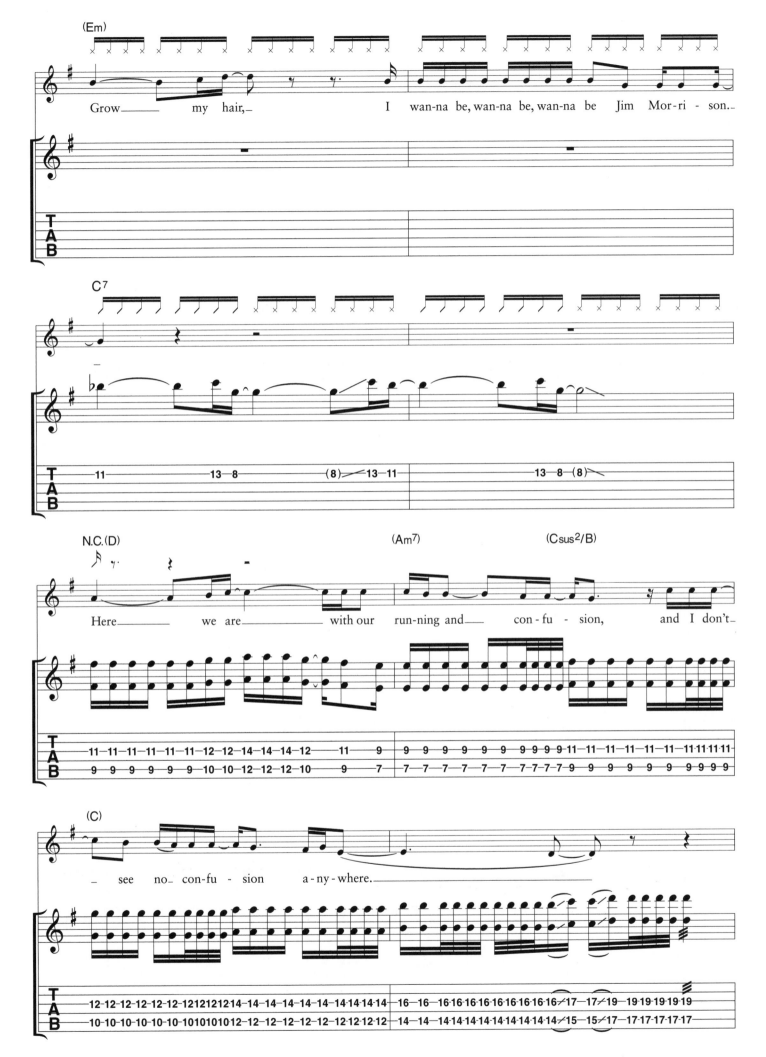

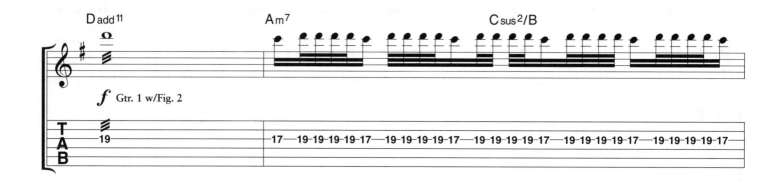

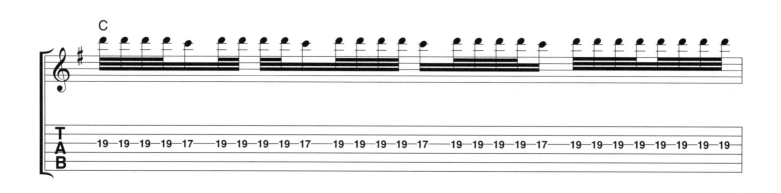

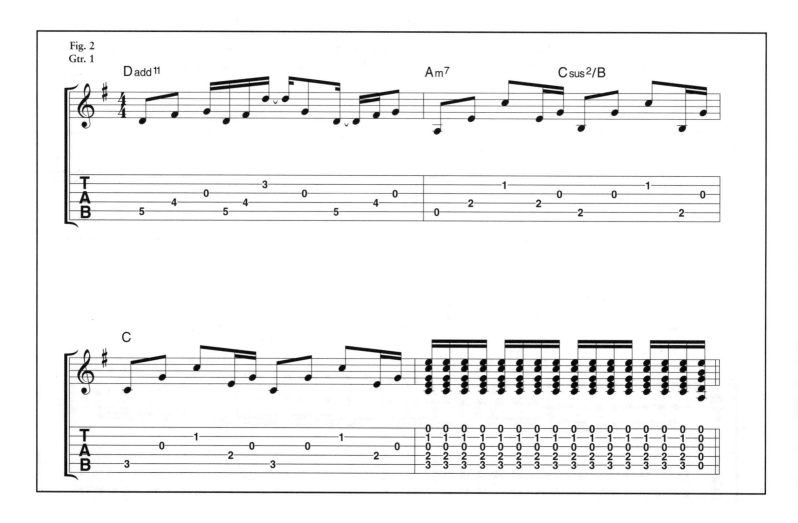

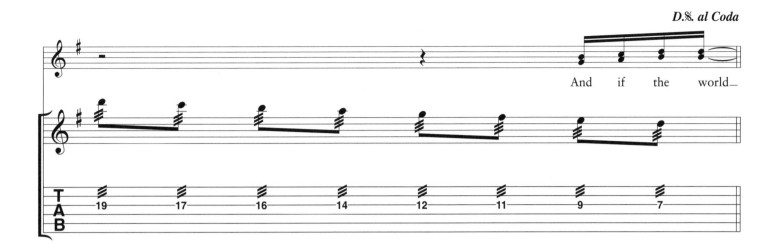

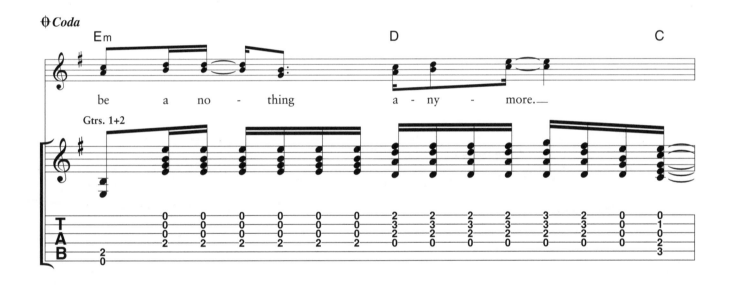

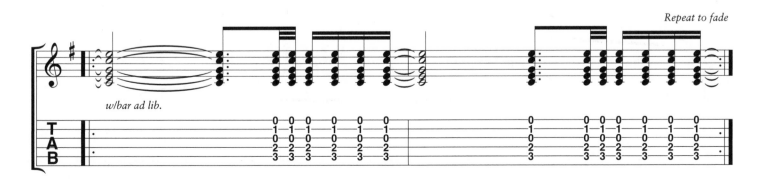

Creep

Words and Music by
THOMAS YORKE, EDWARD O'BRIEN, COLIN GREENWOOD, JONATHAN GREENWOOD,
PHILIP SELWAY, ALBERT HAMMOND AND MIKE HAZELWOOD

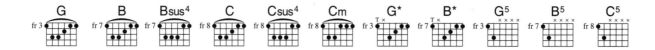

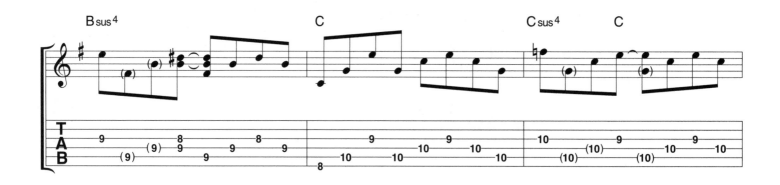

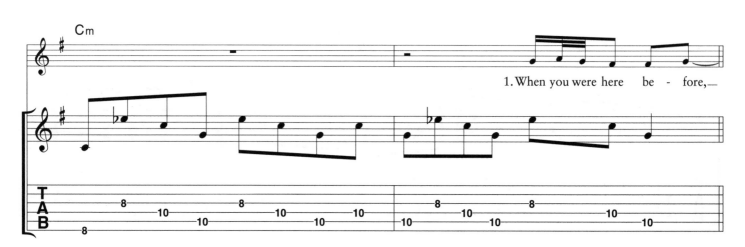

1.When you were here be - fore,—

Verse:

I wish I was spe - cial,   you're so f***-ing spe -
you're so f***-ing spe - cial,   I wish I was spe -

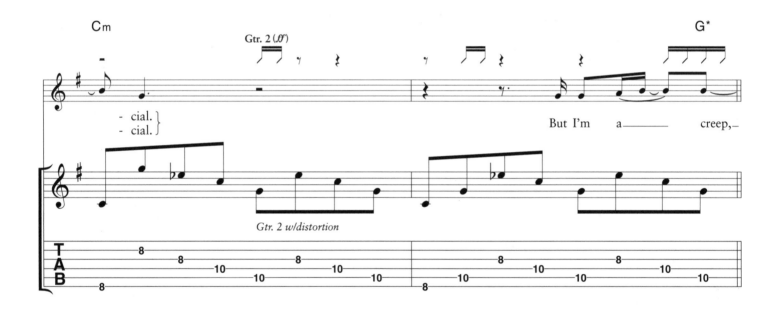

- cial.}
- cial.}

But I'm a_____ creep,—

Gtr. 2 w/distortion

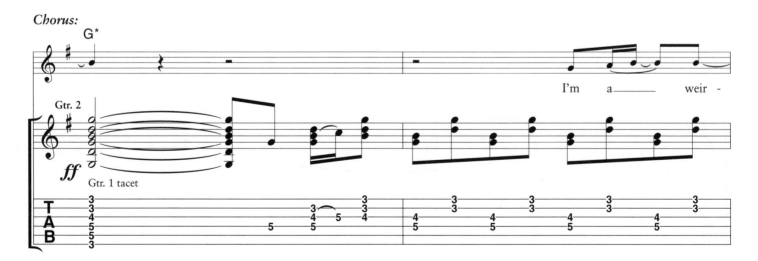

Chorus:

I'm a_____ weir -

Gtr. 2

Gtr. 1 tacet

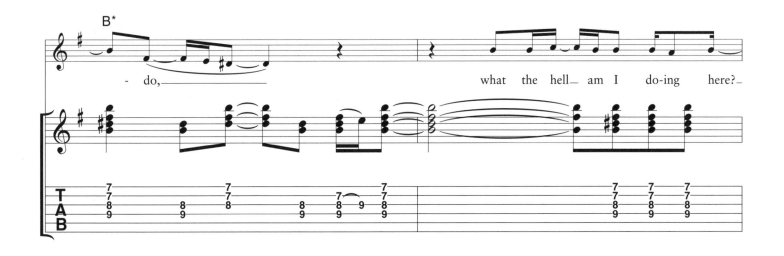

what the hell— am I do-ing here?—

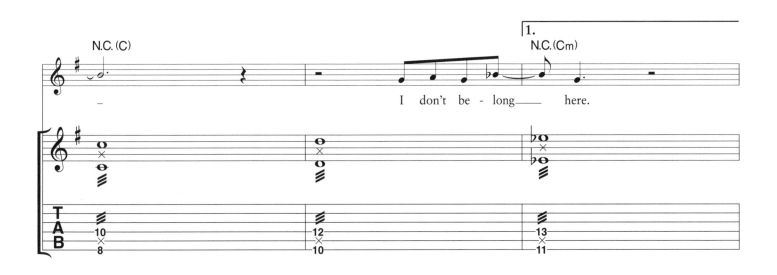

I don't be - long—— here.

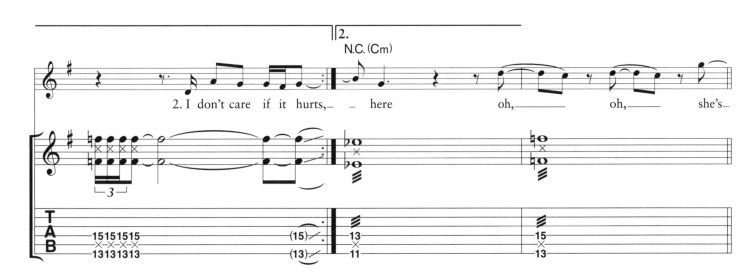

2. I don't care if it hurts,— — here oh,—— oh,—— she's—

Bridge:

I'm a ___ weir - do, ___

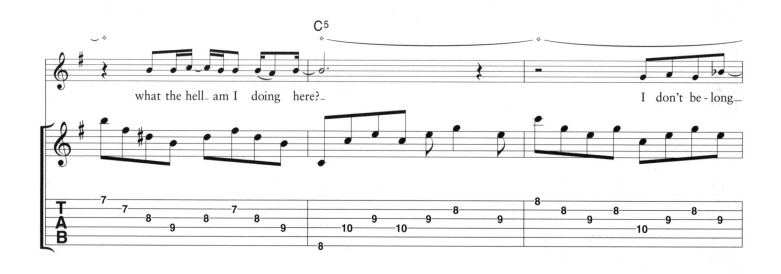

what the hell ___ am I doing here? ___ I don't be - long ___

___ here, I don't be - long ___ here.

Pno. arr for gtr.

Gtr. 1 tacet   *rit.*

Karma Police

Words and Music by
THOMAS YORKE, JONATHAN GREENWOOD, PHILIP SELWAY,
COLIN GREENWOOD AND EDWARD O'BRIEN

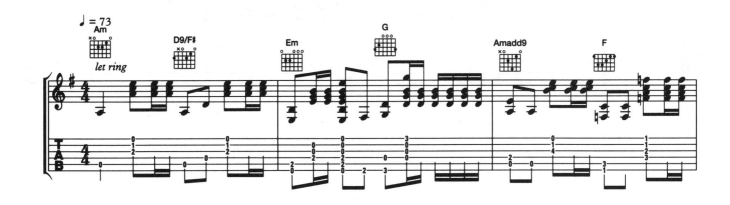

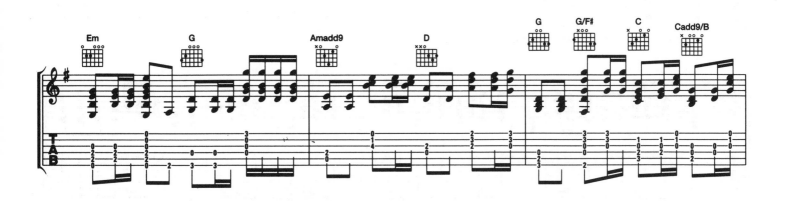

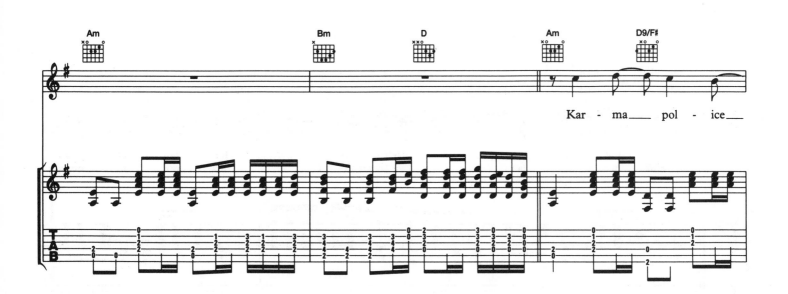

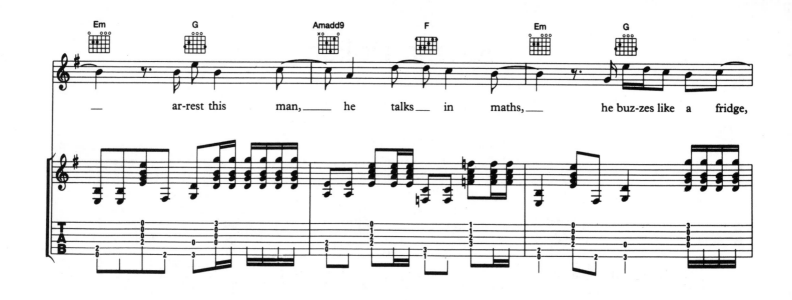

ar-rest this man,____ he talks____ in maths,____ he buz-zes like a fridge,

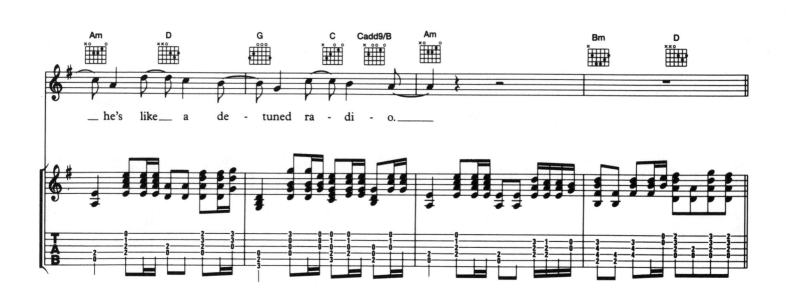

____ he's like____ a de - tuned ra - di - o.____

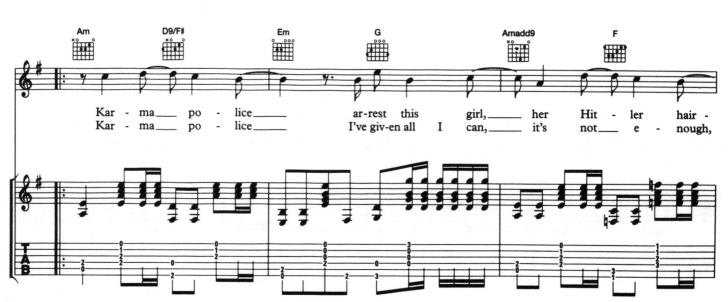

Kar - ma____ po - lice____ ar-rest this girl,____ her Hit - ler hair -
Kar - ma____ po - lice____ I've giv-en all I can,____ it's not____ e - nough,

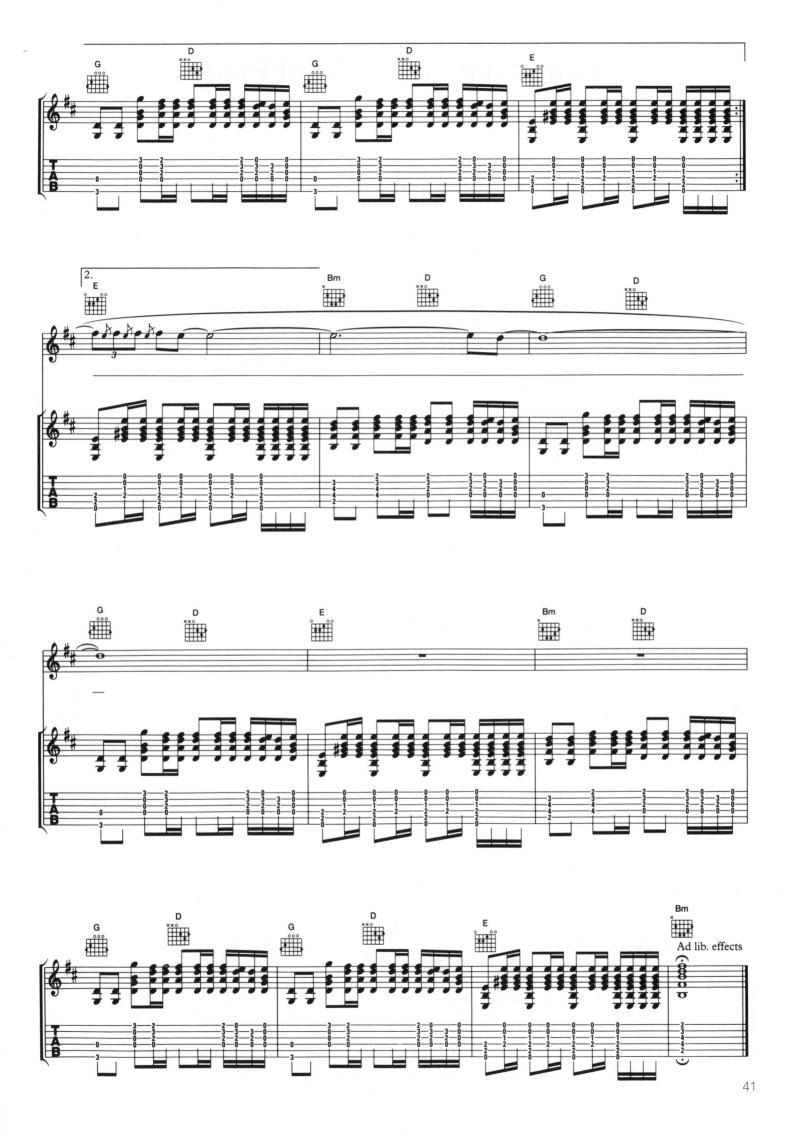

Everything In It's Right Place

Words and Music by
THOMAS YORKE, PHILIP SELWAY, EDWARD O'BRIEN,
COLIN GREENWOOD AND JONATHAN GREENWOOD

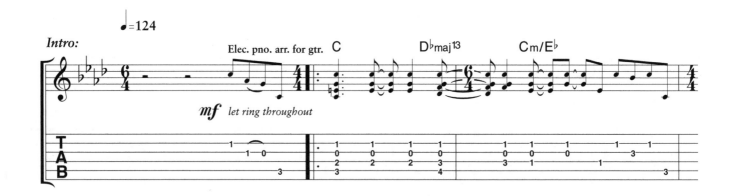

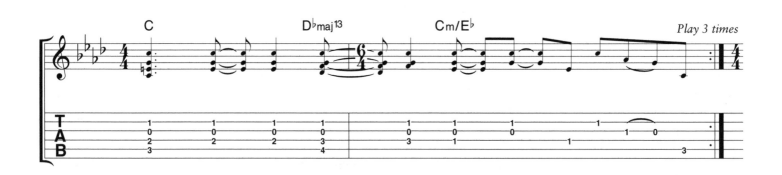

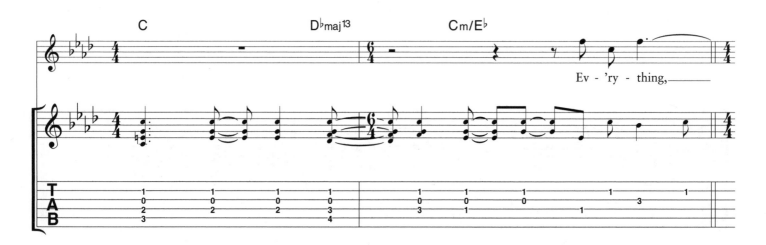

Ev - 'ry - thing,

Chorus:

Verse:

Chorus:

46

Bridge:

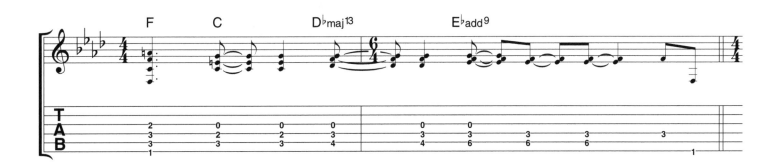

F   C   D♭maj¹³   E♭add⁹

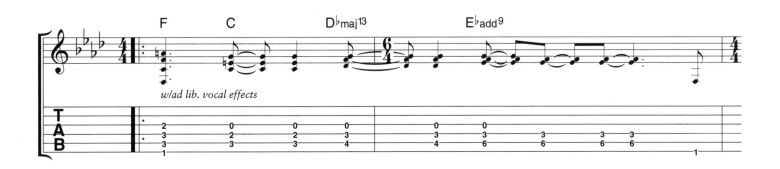

F   C   D♭maj¹³   E♭add⁹

w/ad lib. vocal effects

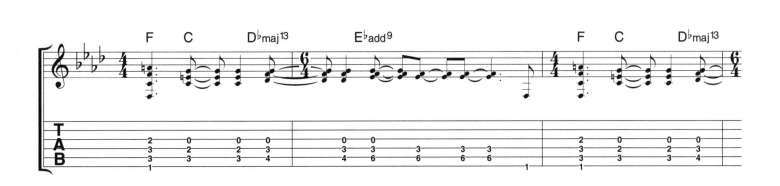

F   C   D♭maj¹³   E♭add⁹   F   C   D♭maj¹³

Repeat ad lib. to fade

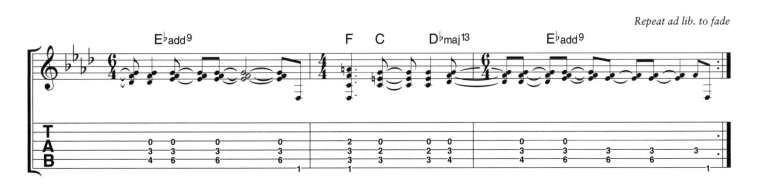

E♭add⁹   F   C   D♭maj¹³   E♭add⁹

Fake Plastic Trees

Words and Music by
THOMAS YORKE, EDWARD O'BRIEN, COLIN GREENWOOD,
JONATHAN GREENWOOD AND PHILIP SELWAY

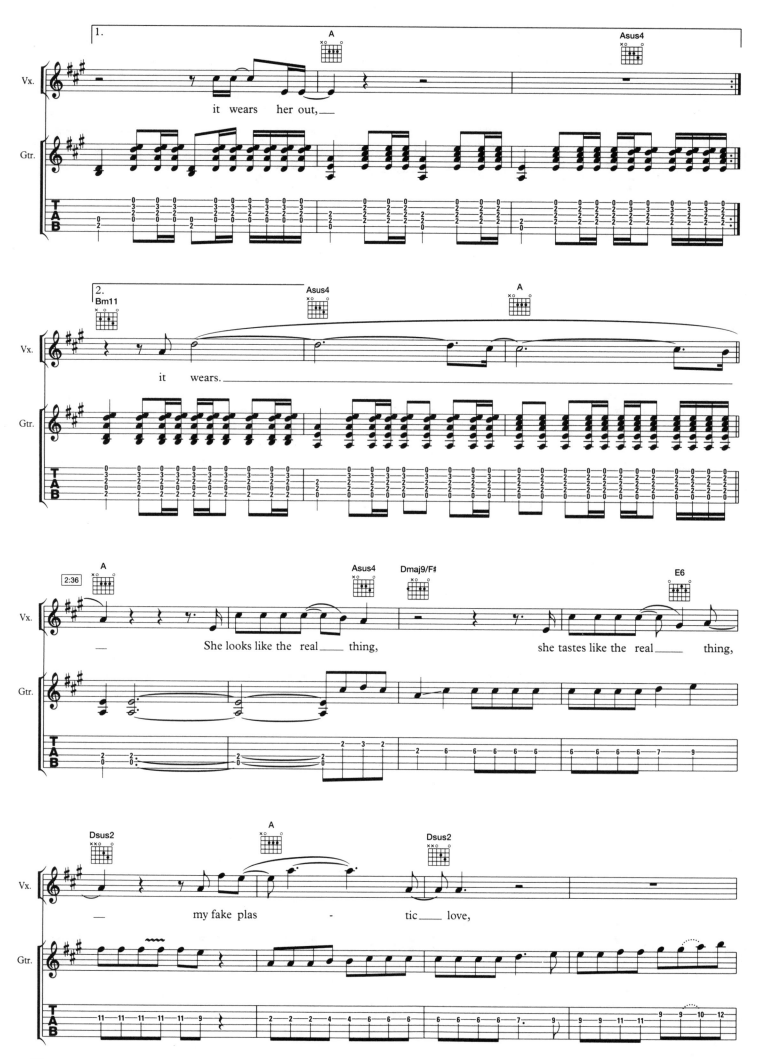

it wears her out,____

it wears.____

She looks like the real____ thing, she tastes like the real____ thing,

____ my fake plas - tic____ love,

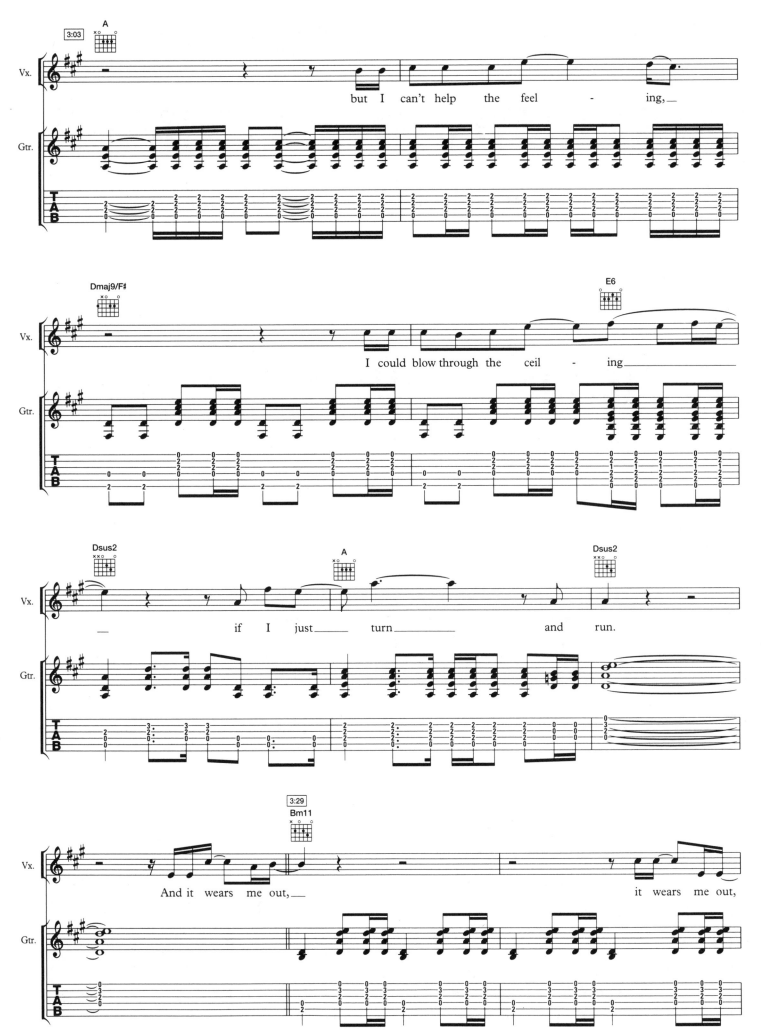

High & Dry

Words and Music by
THOMAS YORKE, EDWARD O'BRIEN, COLIN GREENWOOD,
JONATHAN GREENWOOD AND PHILIP SELWAY

don't leave me____ dry.____

don't leave me dry. ____

let ring

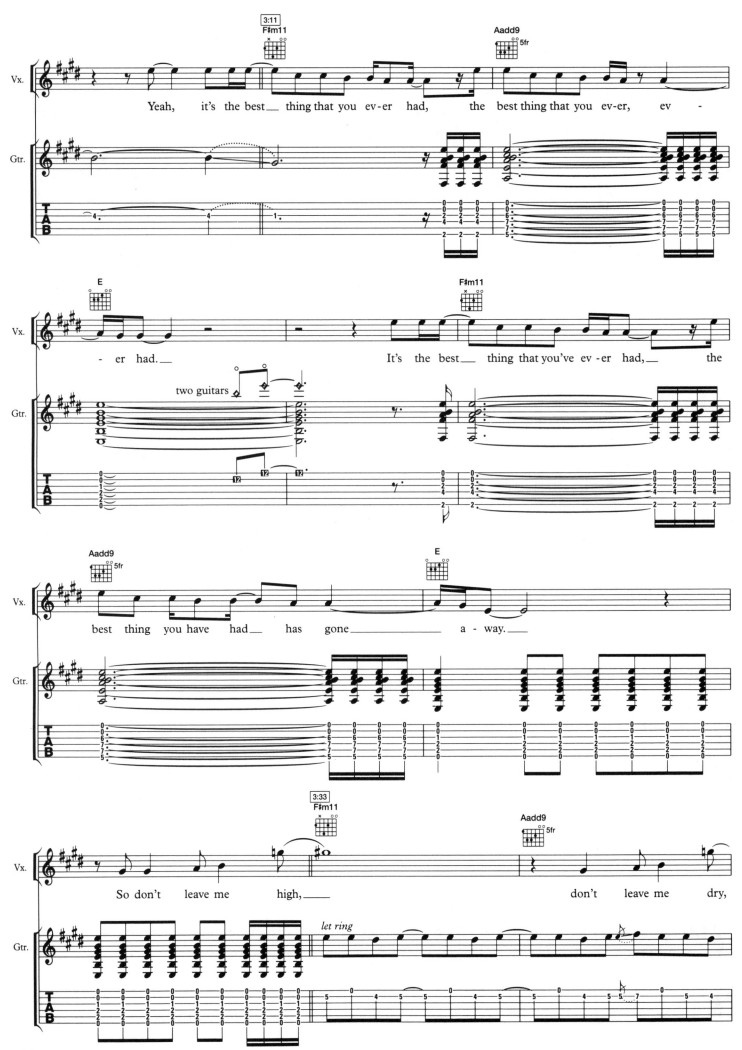

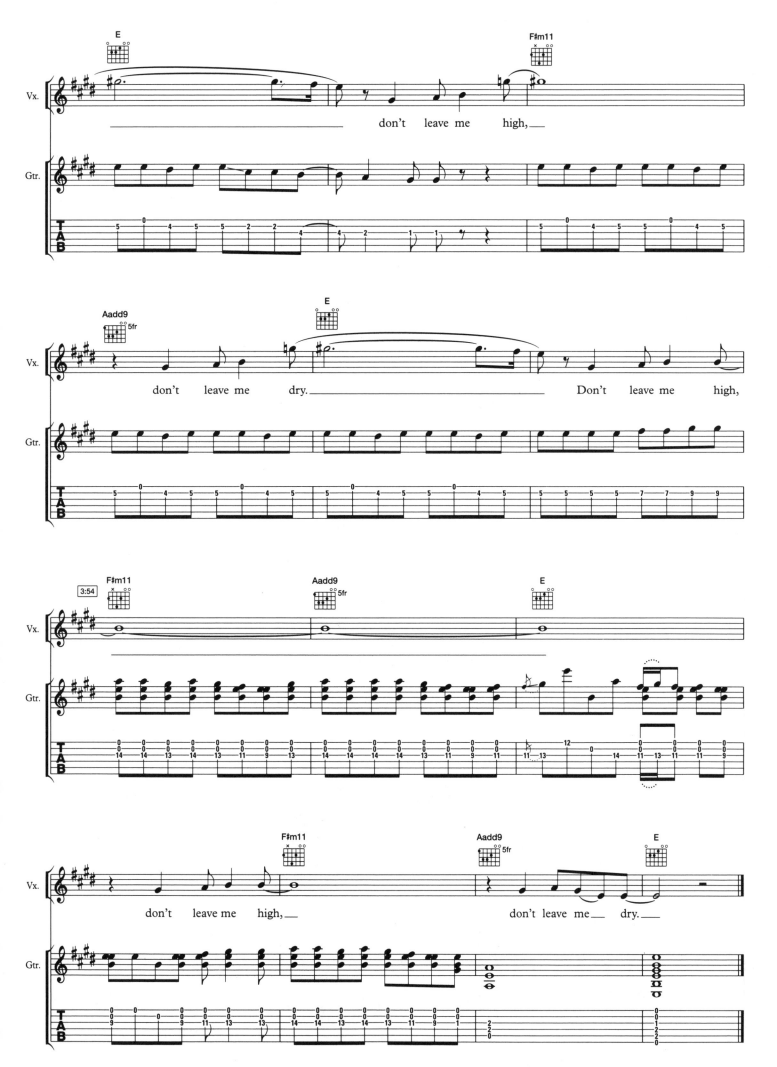

Just

Words and Music by
THOMAS YORKE, EDWARD O'BRIEN, COLIN GREENWOOD,
JONATHAN GREENWOOD and PHILIP SELWAY

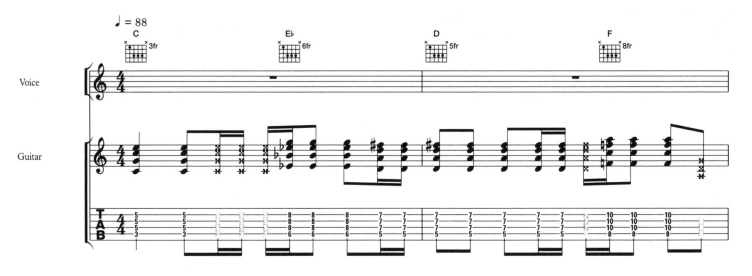

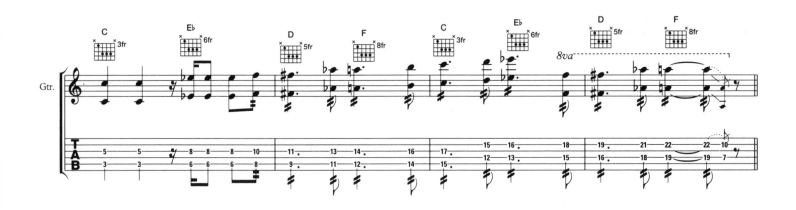

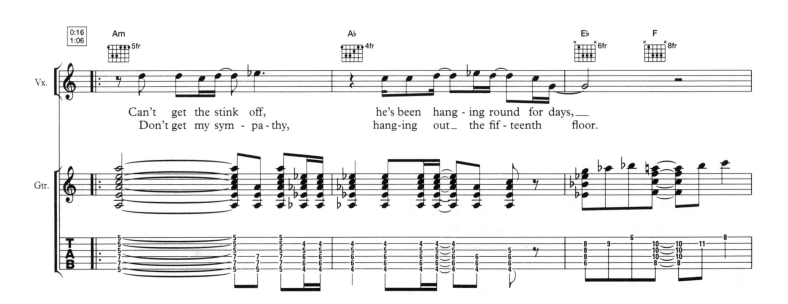

Can't get the stink off, he's been hang-ing round for days, ___
Don't get my sym-pa-thy, hang-ing out ___ the fif-teenth floor.

comes like a com - et,
You've changed the locks three times,
suck-ered you, but not your friends.
he still comes reel - ing through the door.

One day he'll get to you,
One day I'll get to you,
and teach you how to be a ho - ly cow.
and teach you how to get to pur - est hell.
You do it to your-

- self, you do, and that's what real - ly hurts is you do it to your-

- self, just you, you and no - one else, you do it to your - self,

65

You do it to your- self,___ you do,___ that's what real-ly hurts is you do it to your-

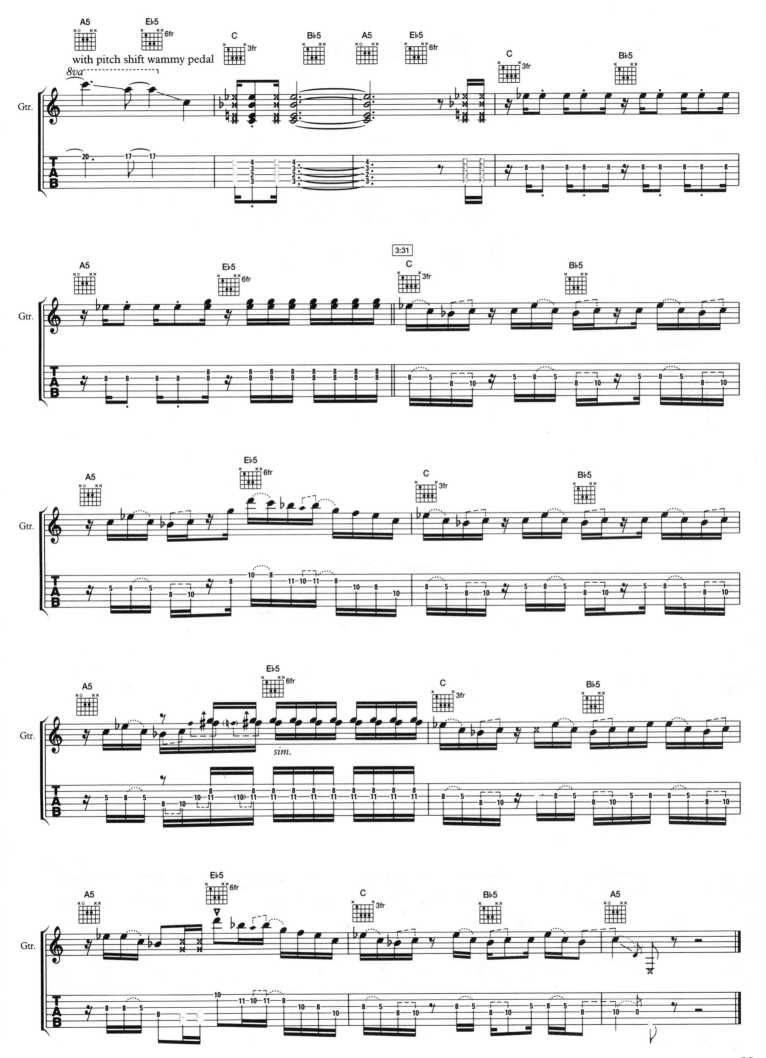

Knives Out

Words and Music by
THOMAS YORKE, JONATHAN GREENWOOD, EDWARD O'BRIEN,
PHILIP SELWAY and COLIN GREENWOOD

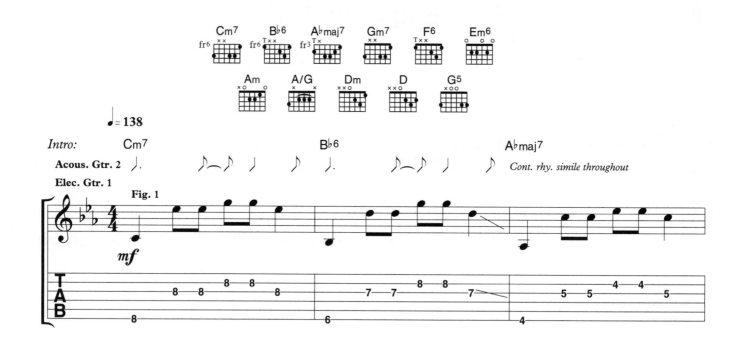

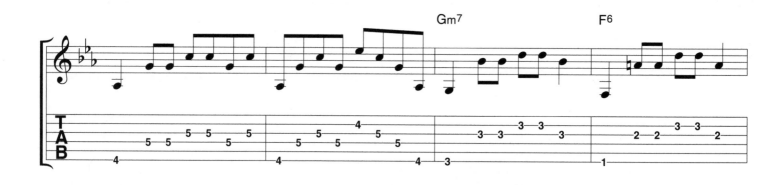

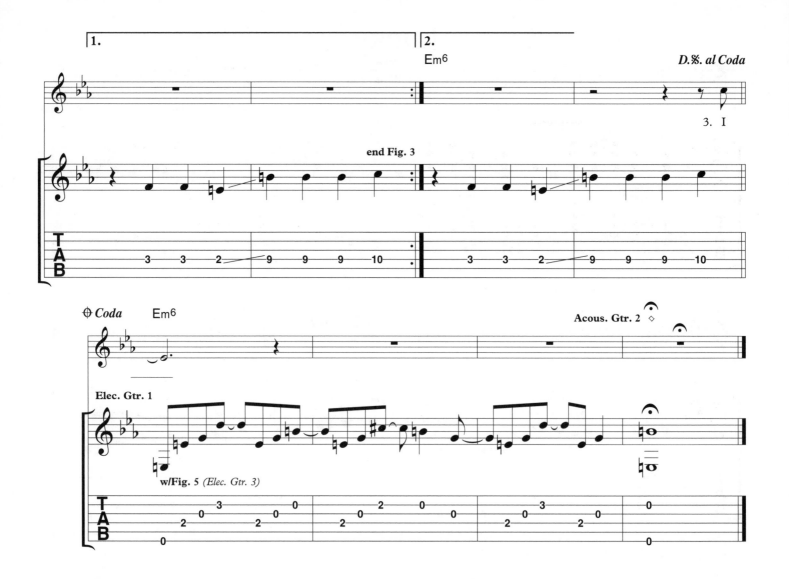

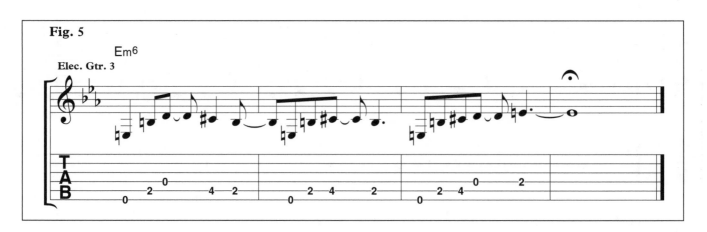

Verse 3:
I want you to know
He's not coming back
He's bloated and frozen
Still there's no point in letting it go to waste.

Lucky

Words and Music by
THOMAS YORKE, EDWARD O'BRIEN, COLIN GREENWOOD,
JONATHAN GREENWOOD and PHILIP SELWAY

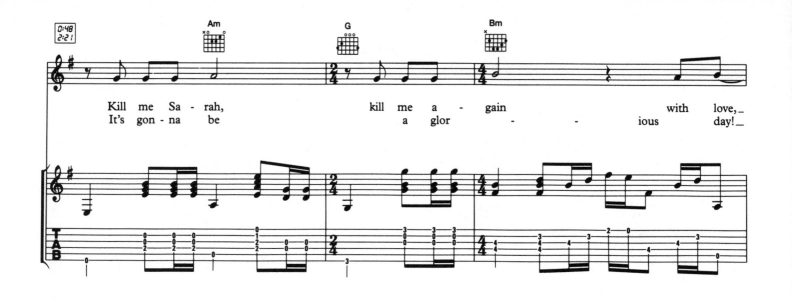

Kill me Sa - rah,   kill me a - gain   with love,_
It's gon - na be   a glor - - - ious   day!_

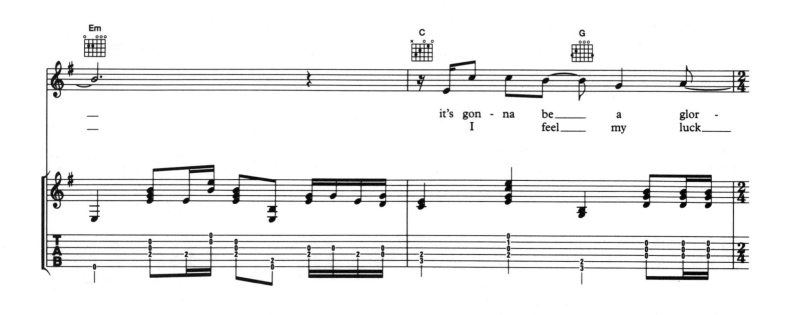

—   it's gon - na be___ a glor -
—   I feel___ my luck___

- ious   day._____   Pull me___ out__
_ could   change._____

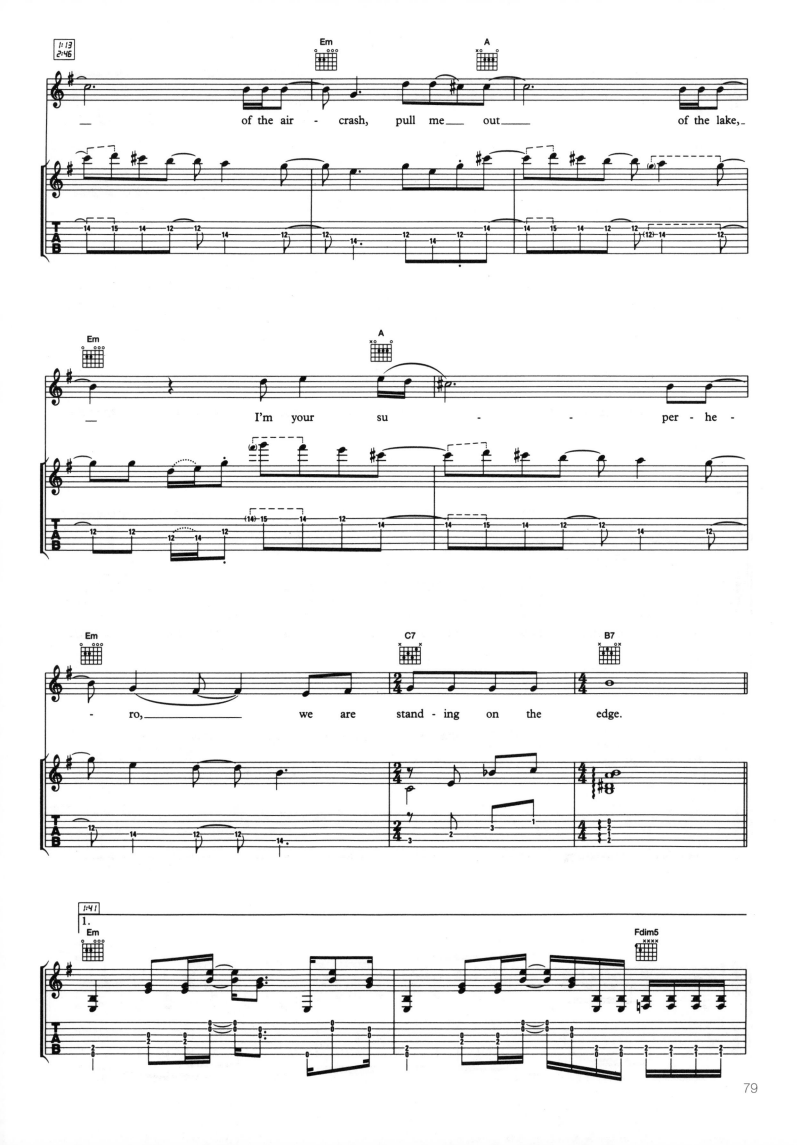

of the air - crash, pull me___ out___ of the lake,___

I'm your su - - - per - he -

-ro,_____ we are stand - ing on the edge.

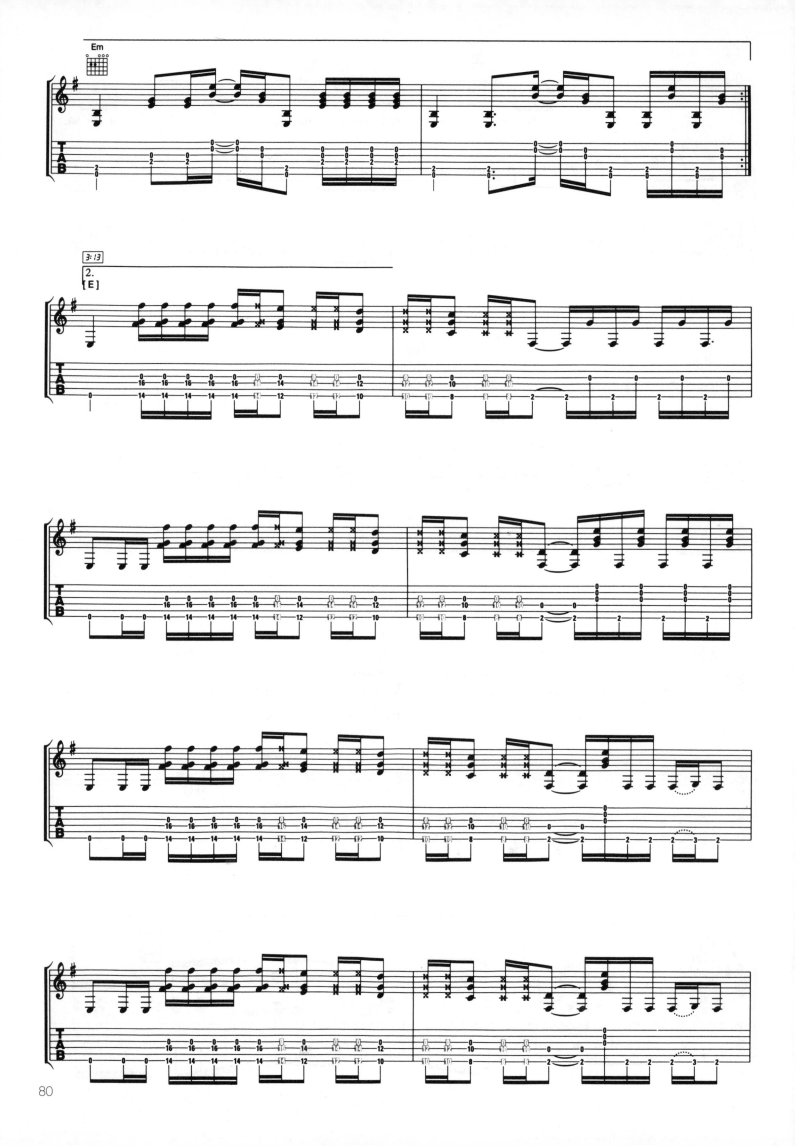

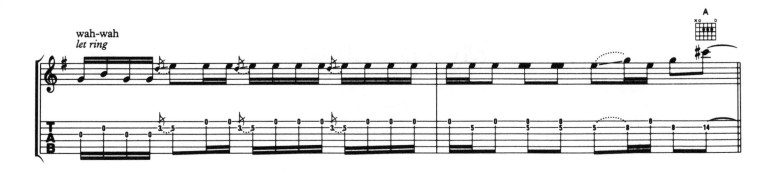

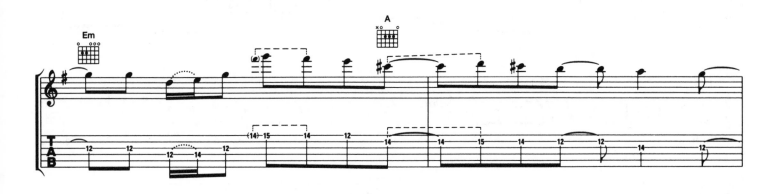

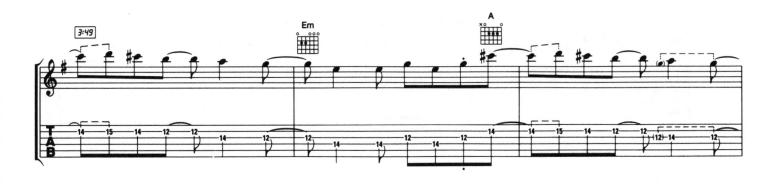

We   are   stand - ing   on   the   edge.

My Iron Lung

Words and Music by
THOMAS YORKE, EDWARD O'BRIEN, COLIN GREENWOOD,
JONATHAN GREENWOOD AND PHILIP SELWAY

Faith, you're driv-ing me a-way, you do it ev-ery day,

you don't mean it, but it hurts like hell. My

Optimistic

Words and Music by
THOMAS YORKE, PHILIP SELWAY, EDWARD O'BRIEN,
COLIN GREENWOOD AND JONATHAN GREENWOOD

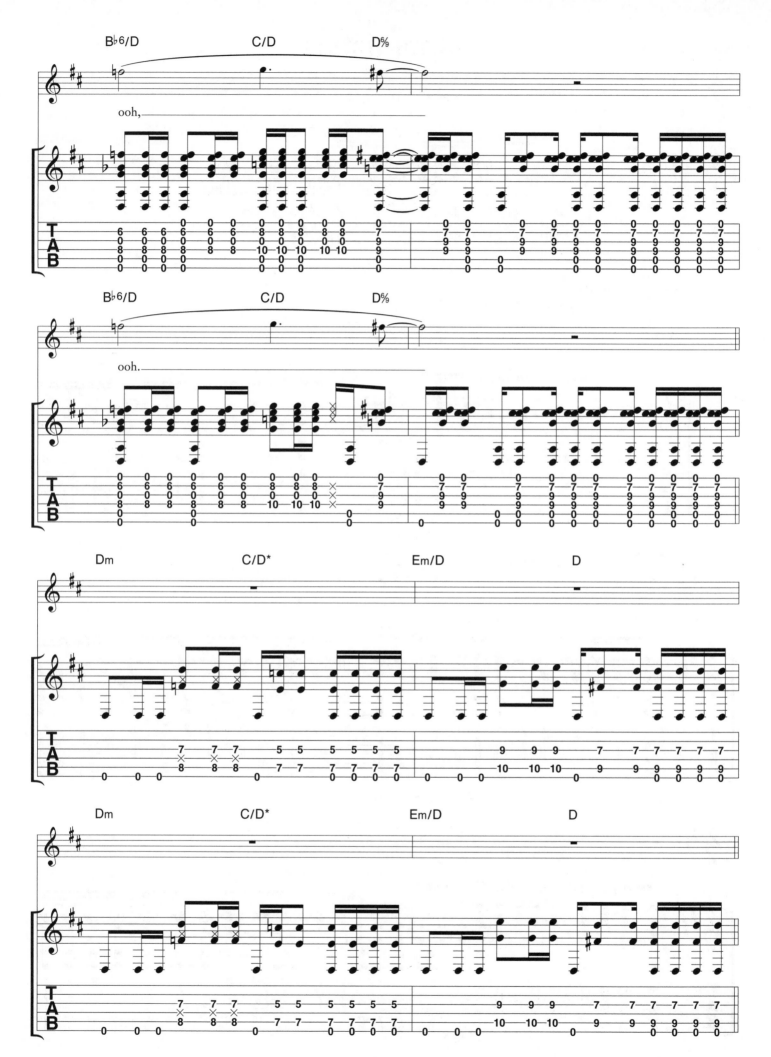

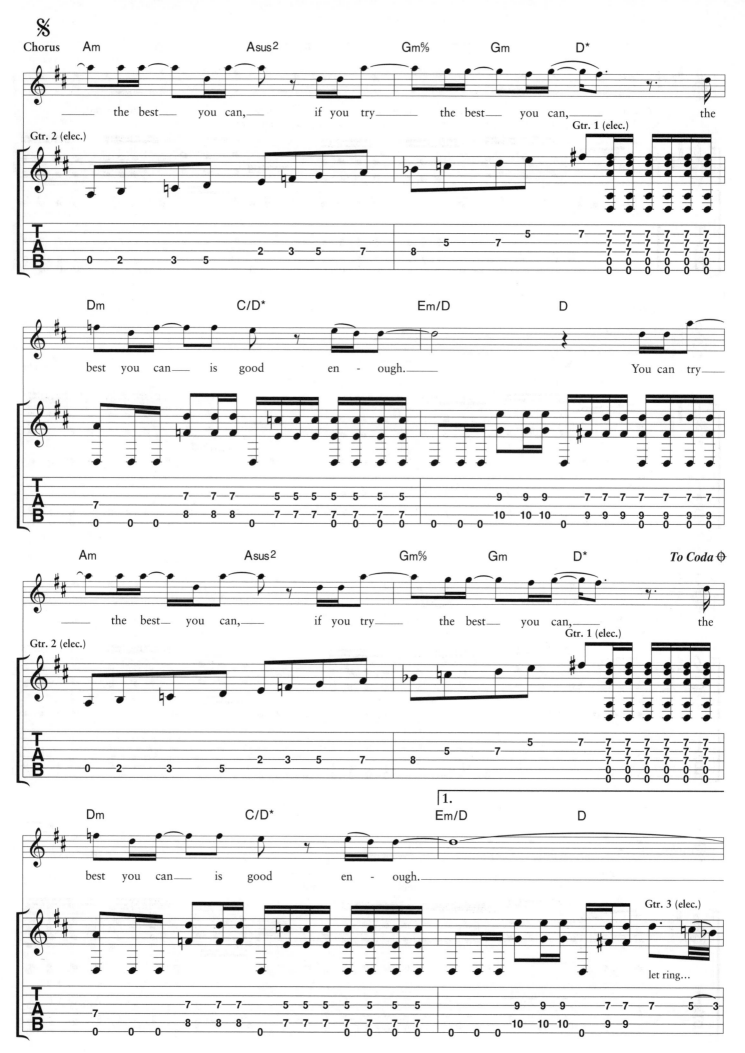

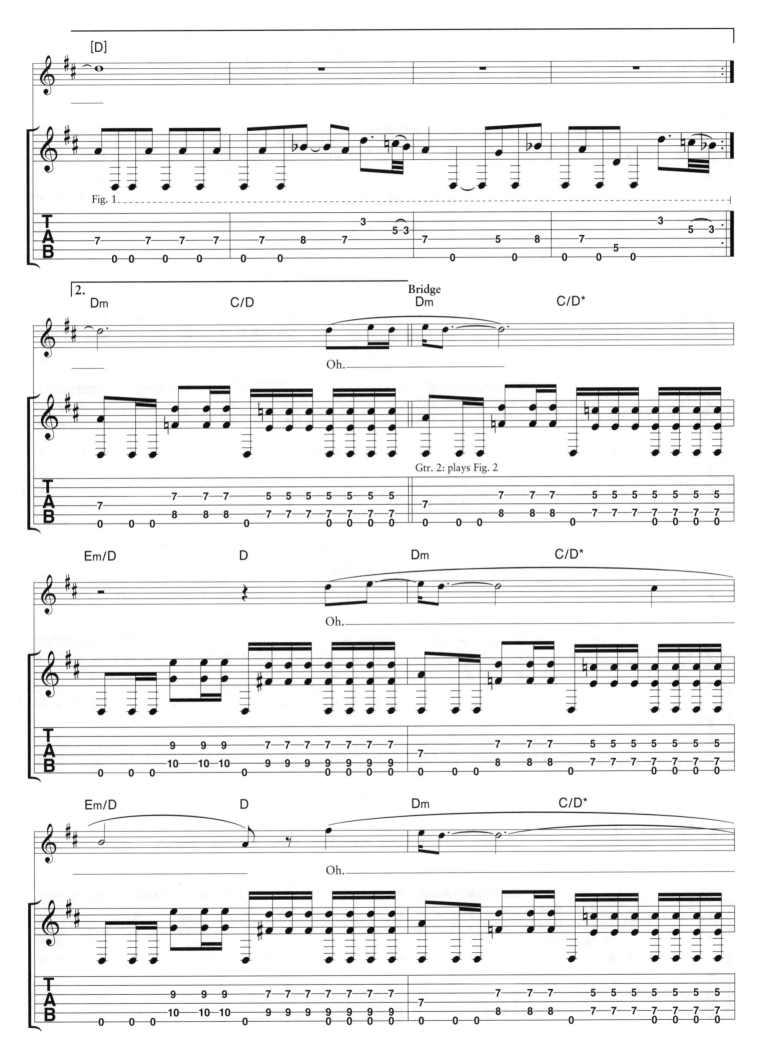

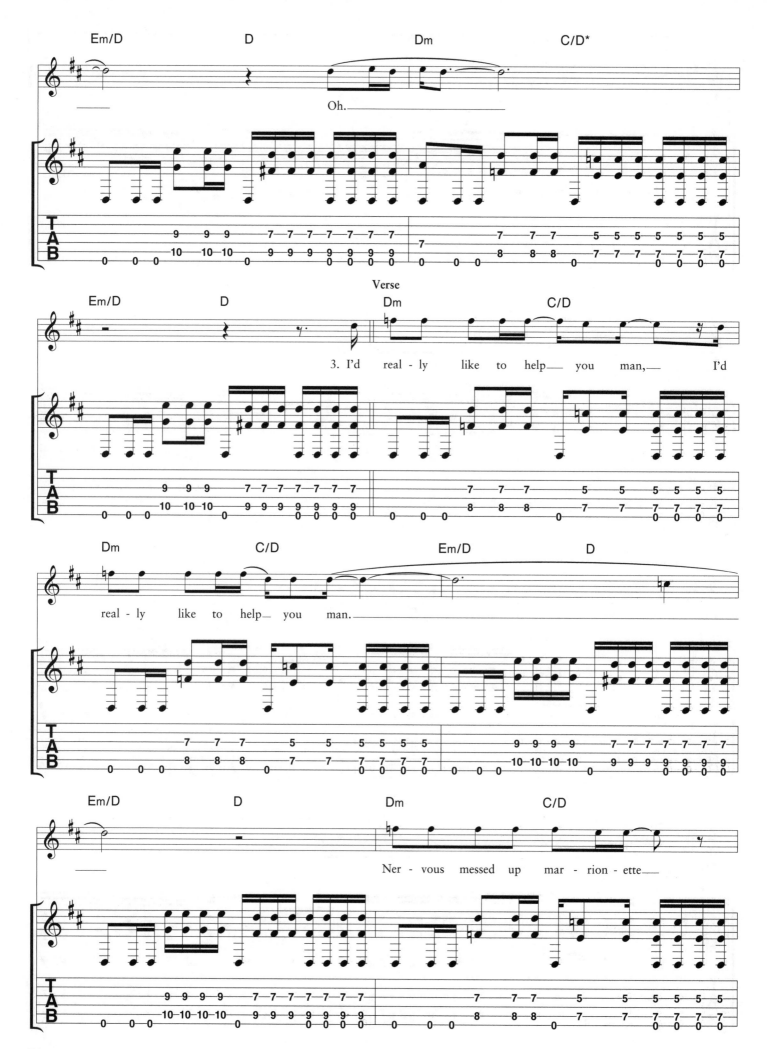

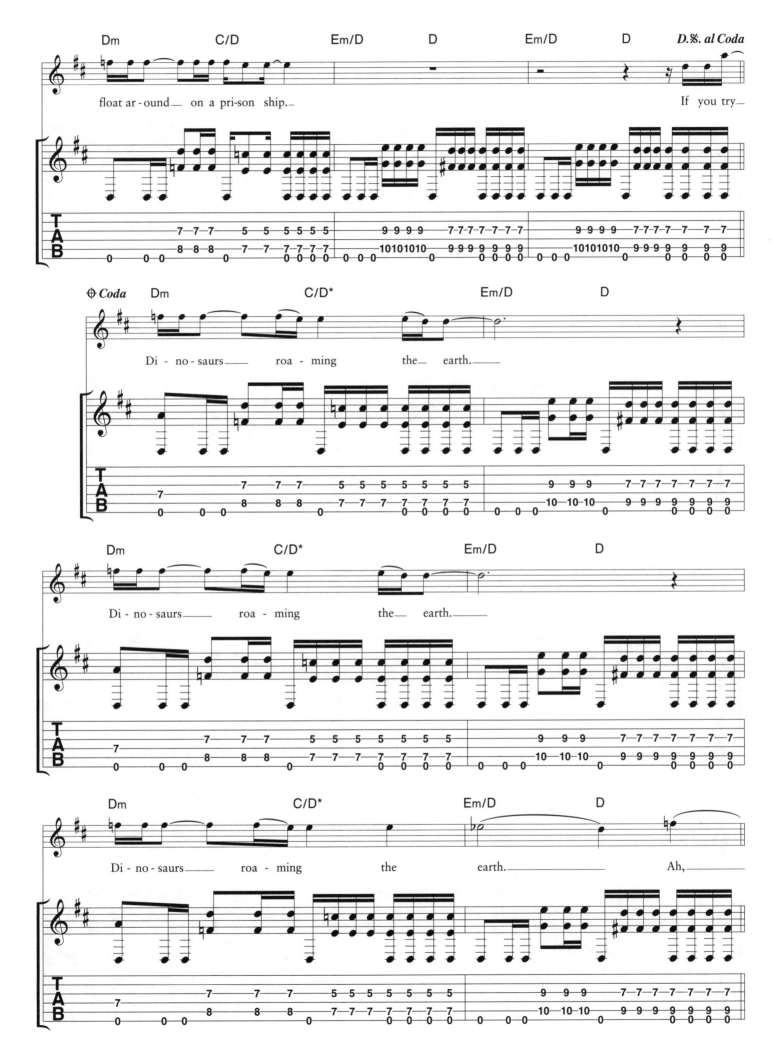

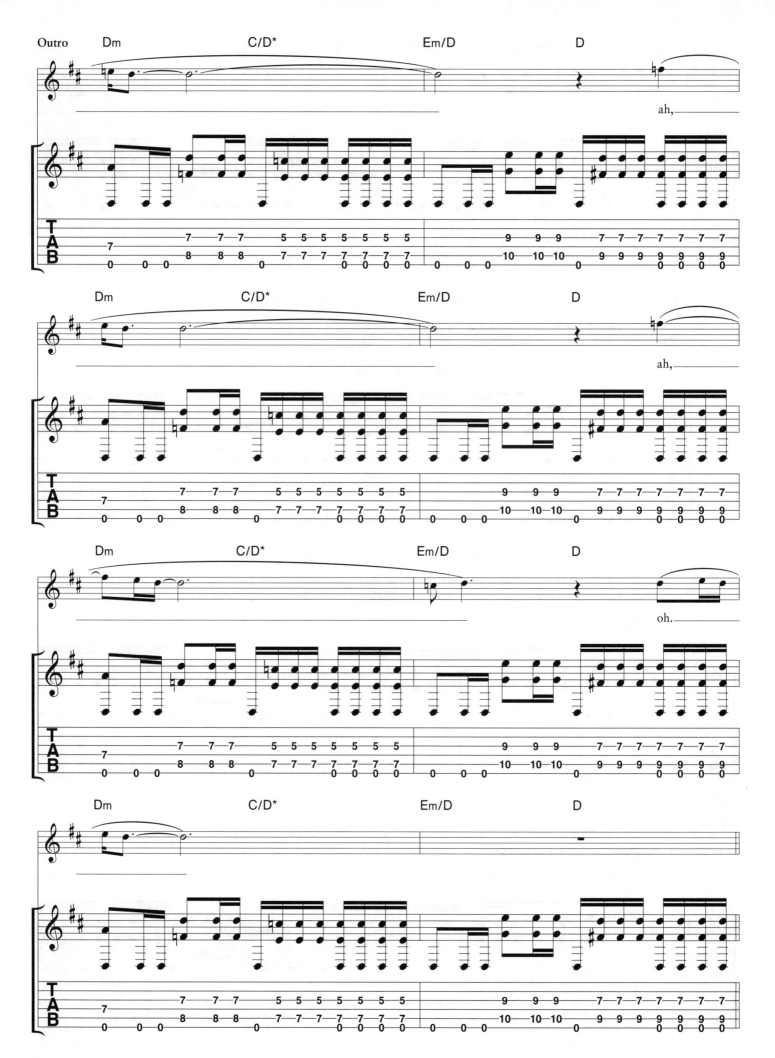

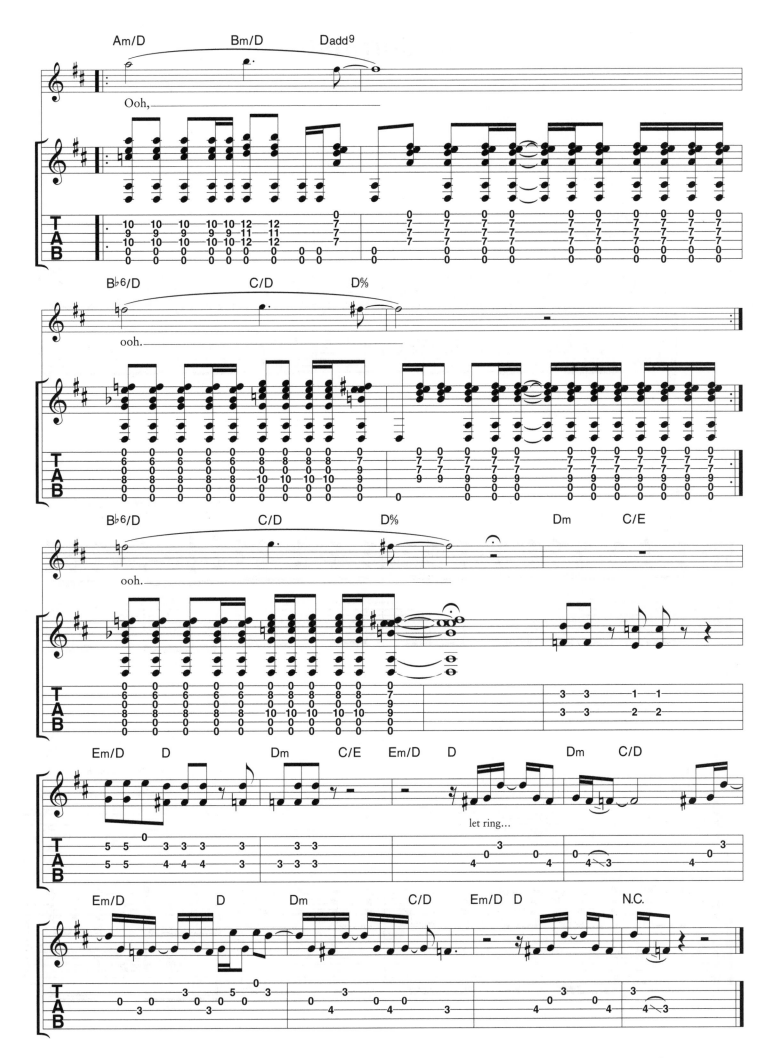

No Surprises

Words and Music by
THOMAS YORKE, JONATHAN GREENWOOD, PHILIP SELWAY,
COLIN GREENWOOD AND EDWARD O'BRIEN

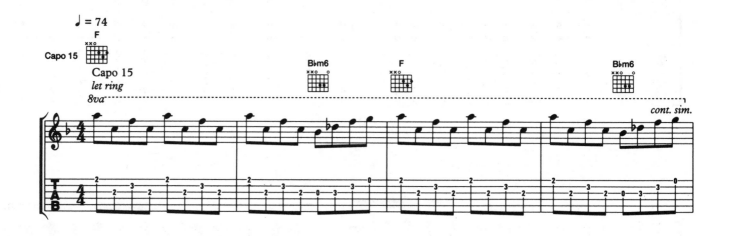

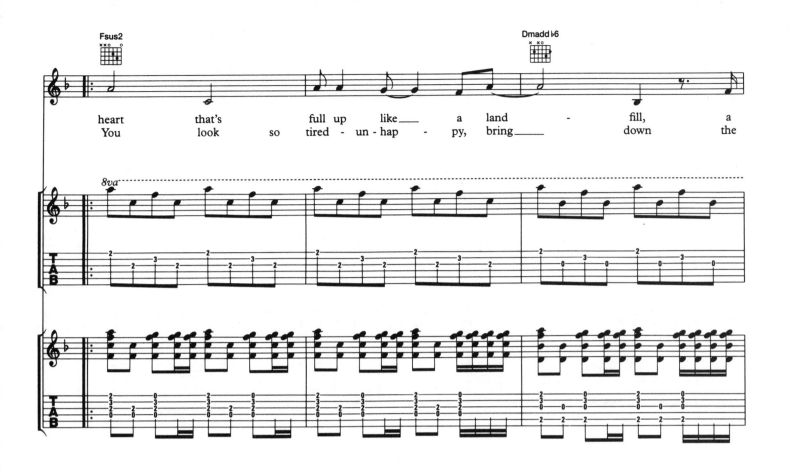

heart that's so full up like___ a land - fill, a
You look so tired - un-hap - py, bring___ down the

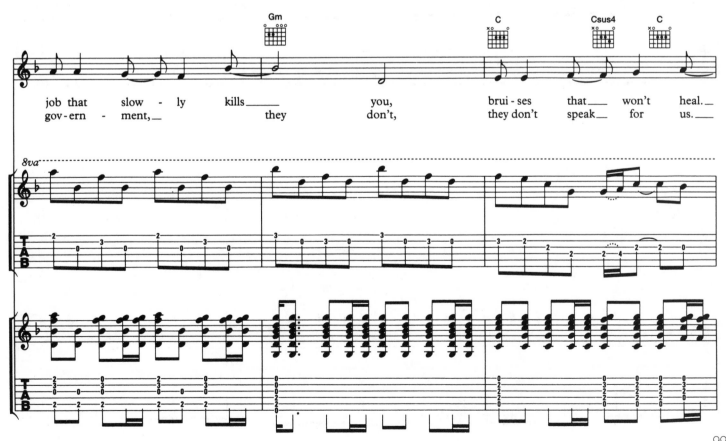

job that slow - ly kills___ you, brui - ses that___ won't heal.___
gov-ern - ment,___ they don't, they don't speak___ for us.___

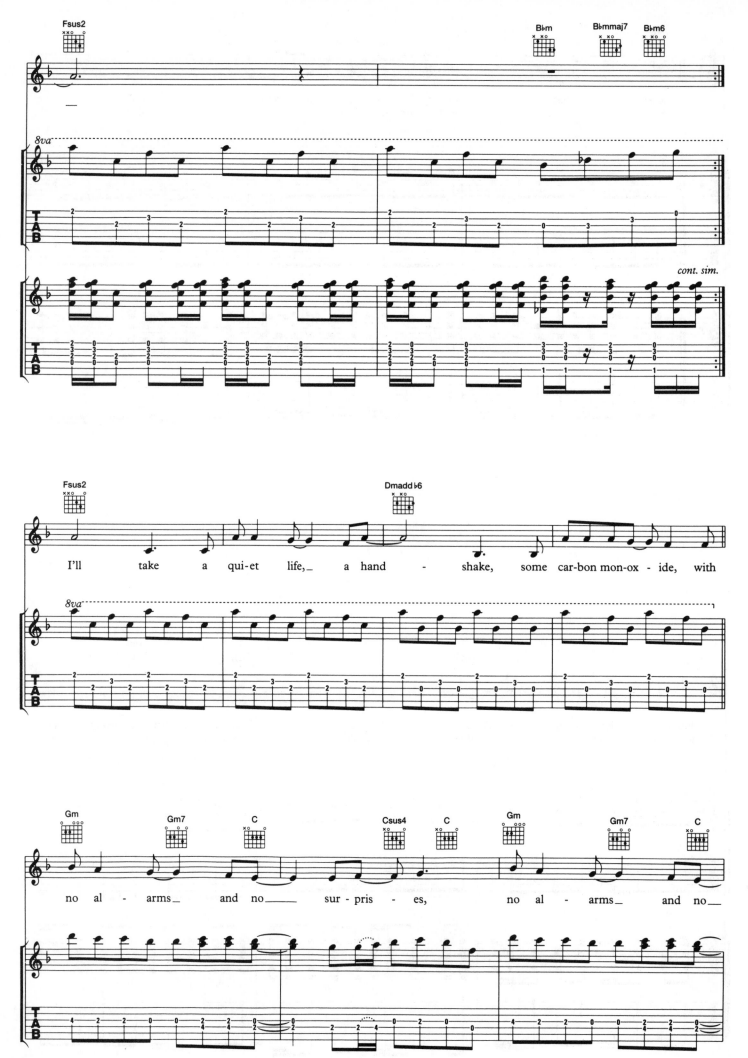

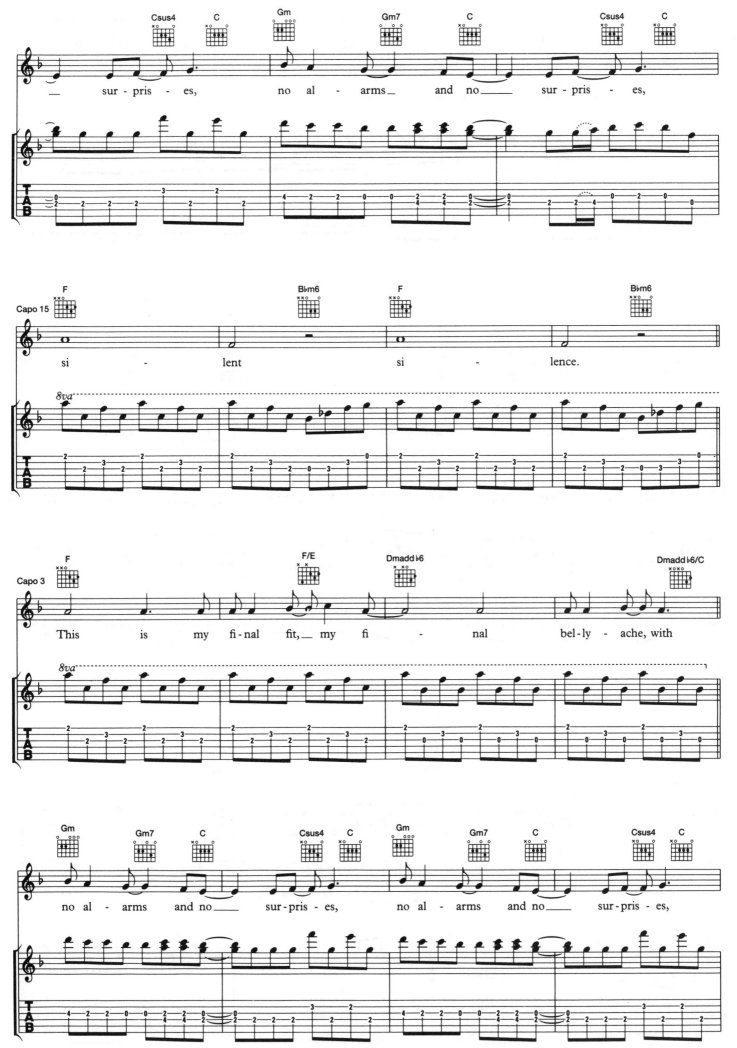

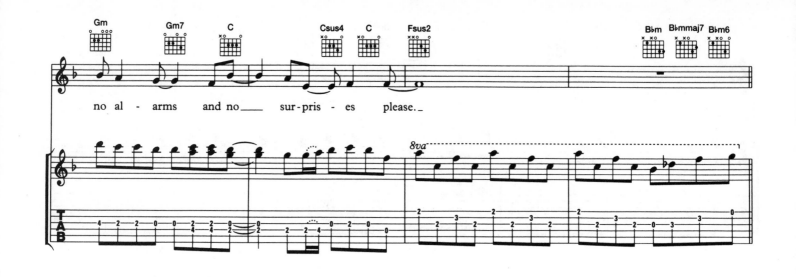

no al - arms and no____ sur - pris - es please.____

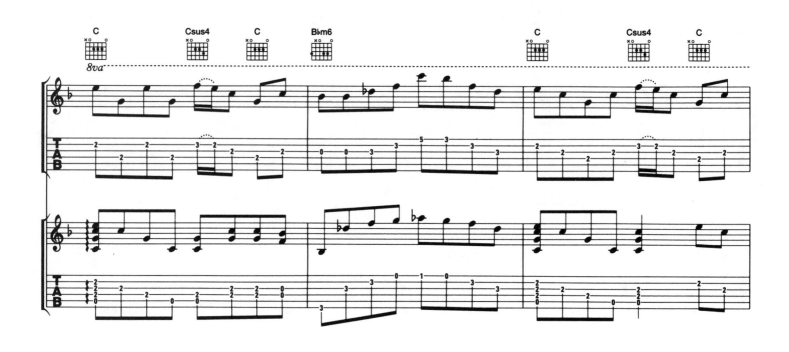

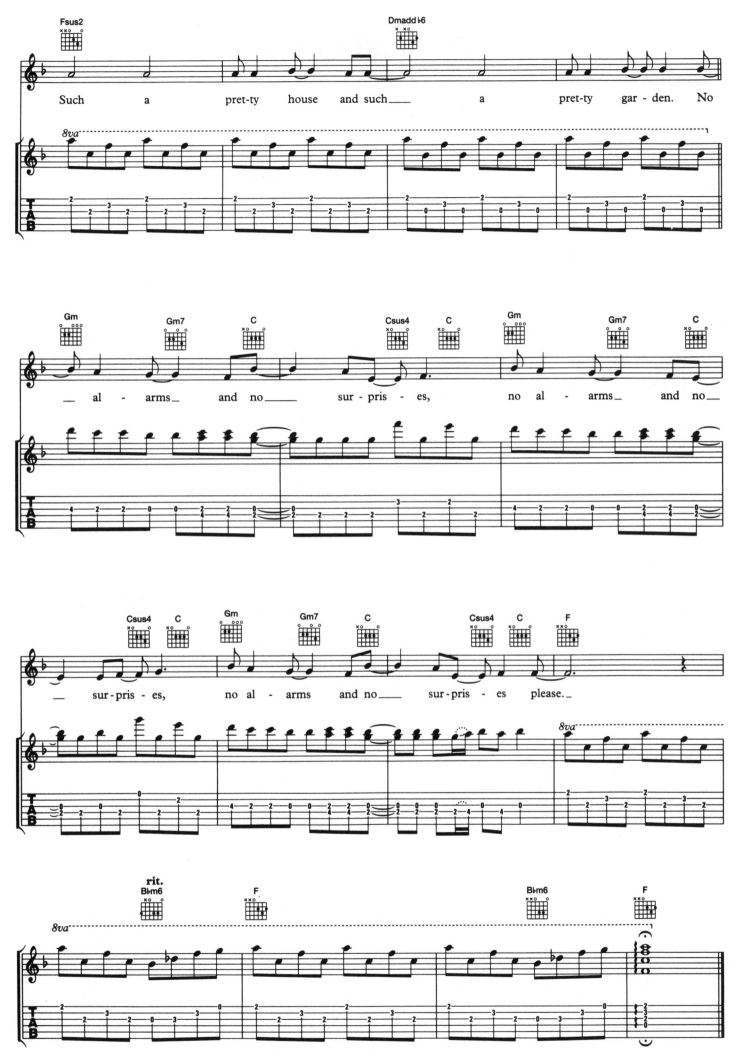

Pyramid Song

Words and Music by
THOMAS YORKE, JONATHAN GREENWOOD, EDWARD O'BRIEN,
PHILIP SELWAY AND COLIN GREENWOOD

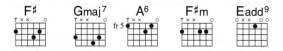

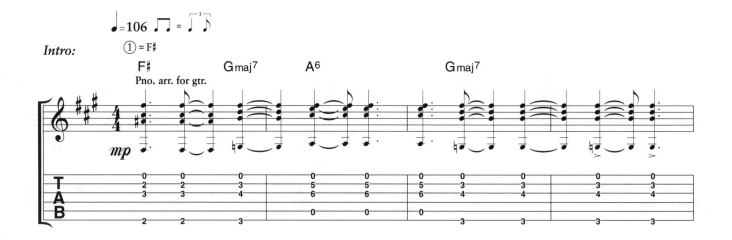

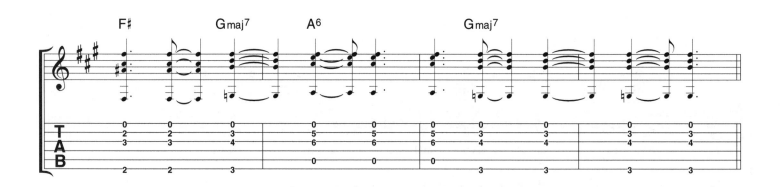

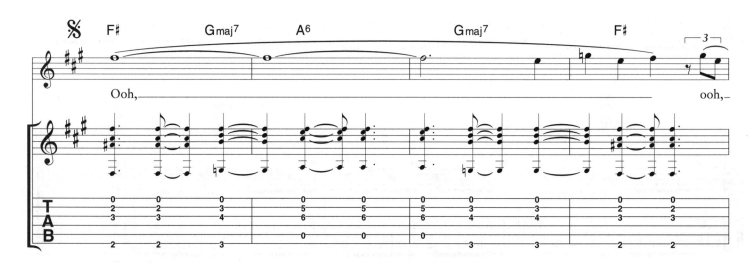

all the fi - gures I used to see.

nothing to fear, no - thing to doubt.

Ooh,

ooh,

ooh.

D.§. al Coda
w/repeats

⊕ *Coda*

1. 2.

no-thing to fear, no - thing to doubt.

There was

Street Spirit

Words and Music by
THOMAS YORKE, EDWARD O'BRIEN, COLIN GREENWOOD,
JONATHAN GREENWOOD and PHILIP SELWAY

Rows of hou - ses all bear - ing down on me,

I can feel their blue hands touch - ing me.